T0082891

SUCH IS THE

Jimmy D. Davis

WestBow Press books may be ordered through booksellers or by contacting:

WestBow Press
A Division of Thomas Nelson & Zondervan
1663 Liberty Drive
Bloomington, IN 47403
www.westbowpress.com
1 (866) 928-1240

ISBN: 978-1-9736-2135-5 (sc)
ISBN: 978-1-9736-2134-8 (e)

Print information available on the last page.

WestBow Press rev. date: 02/22/2018

CONTENTS

Preface.....ix
Introduction.....xi

Chapter 1: Being in the Spirit.....1
Chapter 2: Speaking in Parables.....6
Chapter 3: The Kingdom.....13
Chapter 4: The Old Testament Kingdom.....18
Chapter 5: The New Testament Kingdom.....24
Chapter 6: Mysteries of God.....31
Chapter 7: The Kingdom is At Hand.....45
Chapter 8: Mysteries of the Kingdom of Heaven.....49
Chapter 9: "Like a Little Child".....52
Chapter 10: The Parable of the Sower.....56
Chapter 11: The Parable of the Tares.....63
Chapter 12: The Parable of the Mustard Seed.....68
Chapter 13: The Parable of the Leaven.....72
Chapter 14: The Parable of the Hidden Treasure.....79
Chapter 15: The Parable of the Pearl of Great Price.....82
Chapter 16: The Parable of the Net.....85
Chapter 17: The Parable of the Householder.....89
Chapter 18: The Parable of the Laborers.....93
Chapter 19: The Parables of the Two Sons, the Householder, and the Wedding Feast (Matthew 21:28 – 22:14).....99
Chapter 20: The Kingdom of Heaven Summary.....114

Dedication

I dedicate this work to my precious grandchildren: Kylen, Kamron, Kadi, Ty, Kyson, and Krista. My greatest prayer is that each of you will grow in God's grace and in the knowledge of our Lord and Savior, Jesus Christ, Who said: "Encourage the children to come unto Me, and don't hinder them, for of Such is the Kingdom of Heaven."

PREFACE

Have you ever wondered; just what is *The Kingdom of Heaven*? What is meant by *Kingdom?* Does *Heaven* really exist? Is there really a true *Kingdom of God*? What is *The Kingdom of Heaven* really like?

Some people don't even believe in God, much less in a kingdom ruled by God. In fact, in our world today, a very large percentage of people either don't believe in God, or go through life ignoring Him altogether.

Well, ignoring or rejecting God is to ignore or reject the Truth. In fact, regardless of what people choose to believe or make a priority in life, nothing whatsoever can change the real Truth. God is the One True God, and He is Omnipotent, Omniscient, and Omnipresent. God is the Almighty Ruler of His Kingdom, which is made up of His entire Creation. In other words, God is the Almighty Ruler of the entire universe, including our world and everything in it. That is the Truth, and denying or disagreeing with it won't change it one bit.

In this writing, I am going to share God's real Truth with you regarding His Kingdom: What it is, and what it's like. In fact, as you consider this great Truth, you can discover the Kingdom of Heaven for yourself. You can become a personal part of the Kingdom of God. You see, The Kingdom of Heaven is much more than just a concept: It is a very real place. The Kingdom of God is much more than just a concept: It is a very real existence. And the real truth is: You can either be a part of it, or apart from it. It's your choice.

INTRODUCTION

By far the greatest authority on the subject of *The Kingdom of Heaven* is the one person who came directly from there to be on this earth and live a life as a human being, while being fully Divine and Holy in His Nature. Of course, I'm speaking of Jesus Christ, God in the flesh, Who came from Heaven down to earth to dwell among us and to teach us Spiritual things. While teaching and preaching the good news of eternal life and salvation being available to anyone who just accepts it, Jesus taught about the specifics of *The Kingdom*.

For anyone willing to listen and learn, Jesus clarified just what Heaven really is, and what it is like. He spoke of "heavenly", or "spiritual" things, which requires a spiritual nature just to understand it. Therefore, it is going to be critical to understand one extremely crucial point: YOU MUST BE BORN AGAIN!

What do I mean by that? Well, as we get into the Truth and profound wisdom of God's Word, you will learn this one great secret of ETERNAL LIFE and THE KINGDOM OF HEAVEN: YOU MUST BE BORN AGAIN!

You see, being born again means being born of the Spirit. In order to understand the things of the Spirit, you must be able to relate to things of the Spirit. In order to relate to God and His Spirit, you must be born again of the Spirit of God. As Jesus Christ Himself tells us in His Word: "God is a Spirit, and anyone who wants to worship Him must worship Him in Spirit, and in Truth" (John 4:24). I've heard about "Quantum Physics" but I really can't relate to it, because I don't have a mind for it and really can't understand it, so I don't even try.

So, in order to understand the Truth about the Kingdom of God and The Kingdom of Heaven, you must understand the things of the Spirit. In order to understand the things of the Spirit, you must have a Spirit. In order to have a Spirit, you must be born of the Spirit. That is what is meant by being BORN AGAIN. Once you have your Spirit, you will be able to fully understand the secrets of the Kingdom.

Much of what Jesus Christ teaches us about the Kingdom is presented in the format of *parables*. A *parable* is a story using real life examples and illustrations to relate Spiritual Truths. Christ was the true Master of using the parable in His teaching. He would give a true life example or relate a true life incident, and then use it to illustrate the Spiritual Truth of the Kingdom. Christ even declared that the reason He used parables was to present Spiritual Truth to those who were Spiritual and not worldly or of the flesh. The people of the world, who were not born again of the Spirit would then not understand the Spiritual Truth Christ presented. In fact, on one occasion, the Apostles who followed and learned from the Lord Jesus, asked Him why He taught in parables. Jesus told them that He spoke in parables so that those rejecting Him wouldn't understand (Matt. 13:10-17).

Do you really want to understand about the Kingdom of God? Do you really want to understand the truths about the Kingdom of Heaven? It's readily available to you: just listen, understand, and believe.

ONE

Being in the Spirit

"Do not marvel that I say to you, you must be born again." (John 3:7)

Perhaps the most important Truth ever shared with mankind came from these words spoken by the Lord Jesus Christ, the ultimate authority on salvation and eternal life. His words were very direct and specific: "You must be born again!" This great Truth comes to us directly from an encounter Christ had with a religious leader of the Jewish people named Nicodemus. Nicodemus was one of those religious people who really thought he was right, when he was actually far from it. Like his fellow Pharisees and pious religious colleagues, Nicodemus lived a religious lifestyle, but had a heart of unbelief and rejection of the Truth of God. He just didn't understand the things of the Spirit. Why: Because he had no Spirit. He had never been born again of the Spirit; an absolute requirement for any individual desiring to have eternal life and an on-going relationship with Almighty God as Heavenly Father.

To look back for just a moment: When Adam and Eve sinned against God by disobeying Him in the Garden of Eden, their punishment was death. Their Spirit, that God had given them from the beginning, died. Later, they died physical death also, but the important matter to consider is that they suffered Spiritual death first. Then, every person born into this world following this Spiritual death is born without a Spirit. But the good news is that each and every one of us is able to regain that lost Spirit by being born again by way of our repentance of sin and faith and trust in Jesus Christ as our sacrifice and means of forgiveness.

This is what Jesus means when He tells us, along with Nicodemus: "You must be born again." Well, Nicodemus came to Jesus by night so that his religious colleagues wouldn't see him talking to Jesus. Remember that the Jewish people did not accept Jesus as being the promised Messiah sent from God to offer salvation and Spiritual life to the world. So, Nicodemus came to Jesus in the night and spoke to Him in order to get to know more about Him. Nicodemus said, "We know you are a teacher from God; because no man can do the miracles you do, unless God is with him" (John 3:2)

When Nicodemus spoke to Jesus, the Lord saw him for what he was, just as He sees every person for who and what we really are. There is no fooling God. So Jesus got right to the point. He knew Nicodemus was a false religious leader and had a heart of sin and hypocrisy. When Nicodemus said that he could tell Jesus was a man from God, Jesus said essentially that there was no way Nicodemus could even understand the things of God, much less know anything of the Spirit. Jesus said, "Most assuredly, I say to you, unless one is born again, he cannot see the Kingdom of God" (John 3:3), meaning that the person will not be able to "see" or understand it, and also, will not be able to "see" or be present in it.

Showing his true ignorance, Nicodemus said, "How can a man be born when he is old? Can he enter a second time into his mother's womb and be born?" (John 3:4) Jesus then goes on to explain this amazing Truth to Nicodemus, and to us.

Christ said, "Most assuredly I say to you, unless one is born of water and the Spirit, he cannot enter the Kingdom of God. That which is born of the flesh is flesh, and that which is born of the Spirit is Spirit. Do not marvel that I said to you, you must be born again" (John 3:5-7).

Jesus then continues to reveal great Spiritual Truth to anyone who is willing to listen and apply God's Truth to their life. Christ says,

"The wind blows wherever it will, and you can hear the sound of it, but you cannot tell where it comes from or where it goes. So is every one that is born of the Spirit." Here is another great example of Christ using a real-life illustration to explain and reveal Spiritual Truth.

But, Nicodemus revealed his true lack of spiritual insight when he said, "How can these things be?" Nicodemus, like so many people today, just can't understand it, because it is Spiritual in nature, and not worldly.

Then Jesus asked Nicodemus a most significant question: "What, are you a master, or teacher of religious Israel and don't know these things? Truly, truly I say to you, We speak of the things We do know, and testify to the things which We have seen; and you do not accept Our witness and testimony. If I have told you of earthly things and you don't believe Me, then how will you believe if I tell you heavenly (Spiritual) things? And no man has ascended up to Heaven except He that came down from Heaven; even the Son of Man Who is in Heaven." Again, Jesus spoke to Nicodemus about Spiritual Truths and not earthly things, knowing fully well that he would not understand the Truth of God.

So, the Lord Jesus Christ speaks to each of us regarding Spiritual matters. He speaks in the form of His Holy Spirit, just as He did to Nicodemus. Notice in Verse 11 of John, Chapter 3: Jesus speaks in the first person plural (We and Our). This is important to see and understand. Christ spoke in this term very purposefully. He reminds us here that He is part of the Holy Trinity of God: God the Father, God the Son, and God the Holy Spirit: God in three Persons, existing as One. Christ says to you and me: "We offer you a completely new and eternal life of the Spirit when you are born again," meaning that God the Father, God the Son, and God the Holy Spirit are readily available as the One True God to give us new life; the life of the Spirit that will live forever within the Spiritual Kingdom of God, which includes the Kingdom of Heaven.

Do you really want to understand the Kingdom of God? Then you must be born again of the Spirit, because the Kingdom of God is Spirit. In order to be born again, you must honestly and earnestly repent of the sin in your life. Everyone is sinful, and everyone must repent in order to be forgiven and cleansed from sin. Repent by asking God to forgive you and cleanse you. And, in asking for His forgiveness, remember that you can only receive God's cleansing and forgiveness in the Name of Jesus Christ, Who went to the sacrificial Cross as the perfect Atonement for all sin. The shed Blood of Jesus Christ is the only way to be forgiven. God is Spirit and is perfectly Holy, not allowing any sin to be in His presence, so He recognizes only Jesus Christ and His perfect sacrifice for sin in order to cleanse the impure human being. Only by being born again of the Spirit can a person relate to God and know God as Heavenly Father. Consequently, only by being born of the Spirit can a person fully and clearly understand the things of the Spirit and the Kingdom.

And just how can you know for certain that you are born again of the Spirit? I'm so glad you asked this question. There is a very simple, yet profound process that you must follow in order to have this new birth. God's Truth tells us that Jesus Christ is the Way, the Truth, and the Life, and no one can come to God except by way of faith and trust in Jesus Christ and His sacrificial death on the Cross. In order to be born again of the Spirit, you must believe God's Word as He tells you that Jesus Christ is the only means by which you can have this new life. You must believe God's Word as He tells you that you must have complete faith and trust in Jesus as the Lord and Ruler of your life. You must admit that you are a sinner who has violated God's righteous and Holy laws. You must then repent of your sins, asking God to forgive you and cleanse you from your unrighteousness. You must simply ask God to give you this new life of the Spirit. You must then profess Jesus Christ as your Lord and place your faith completely in Him. After all, it is Christ's sacrifice that God considers when he forgives and cleanses you. Your new Spiritual birth is not dependent on anything you do or any type of merit you have earned for good deeds. You can't do anything good enough to earn God's salvation and Spiritual birth. Jesus Christ did it and earned it on the Cross, and offers His gift of forgiveness to you.

When you do this, you will receive the Holy Spirit of God in your life. The Holy Spirit will come into your life and give you the Spirit God wants you to have. Once you have your new Spiritual life, you will be a new creation, being born into the Kingdom of God, and becoming a true member of the Kingdom of Heaven for all eternity.

It is really that simple and really that profound!

TWO

Speaking in Parables

"Unto you (who are of the Spirit) it is given to know the mystery of the Kingdom of God, but unto them that are outside of the Spirit, all these things are spoken in parables." (Mark 4:11)

To paraphrase Christ's statement: "I speak in parables so they won't understand." And just who are *they*? *They* refers to the people of this world who reject or ignore the Truth of God's Word, and the loving grace of God, as shown by His offering of Jesus Christ as the full sacrifice and payment for all sin. These people are not of the Spirit, but are of the world, and being of the world, are under the influence and power of Satan and sin. In truth, it is God's perfect Will that His Truth be revealed to those who repent of sin and trust in Jesus Christ as Lord and Savior, and not revealed to those of this sinful world who do not believe in Jesus Christ. If you choose to remain a part of this sinful world, ignoring or rejecting Jesus Christ and His forgiveness and salvation, then you will be one of those people who may "have eyes to see, but do not perceive; and have ears to hear, but do not understand." You will simply not understand the things that are Spiritual.

Now, just what is a *parable*? The word *parable* means a similitude or symbolism used as a narrative to convey a moral or spiritual truth. In other words, it is a narrative story using a real life illustration to teach a spiritual or moral truth. Many times, the illustration or narrative is difficult to relate to the real spiritual meaning. That is exactly why Jesus used parables in His teaching: so that everyone that is of the world would not understand, but rather Christ's truly born-again spiritual followers would have the clear meaning.

Many people think that Jesus spoke and taught in parables in order to make His message clear and understandable, but that is not the case. Even the Apostles and disciples that followed Jesus closely and believed in Him, were often confused or unclear as to His real meaning. On several occasions they asked Jesus to explain the parable to them.

So, why would Jesus intentionally use these parables in order to confuse some of the people? As Christ told us, the secrets or mysteries of the Kingdom of God are not for the understanding of the world and sinful people. The mysteries of the Kingdom of God are for the understanding of God's children who have been born again of the Spirit, and are therefore members of the Kingdom, by being members of God's Spiritual Family.

In the Gospel accounts of Matthew, Mark, Luke, and John, we see Jesus using parables to teach His Spiritual Truths. "All these things spoke Jesus unto the multitude in parables; and without a parable spoke He not unto them" (Matthew 13:34). "But without a parable spoke He not unto them" (Mark 4:34). "This parable spoke Jesus unto them; but they understood not what things they were which He spoke unto them" (John 10:6).

There are eight parables found in the Gospel of Matthew, Chapter 13. In some studies of the Bible you will see reference to the seven parables of the Kingdom, but at the end Christ tells another short parable with a different application. So we will consider these eight parables in our study initially.

And so, Jesus used parables often for His Divine purpose, which was to reveal the Spiritual Truth to those who believed and trusted in Him, and to keep the Truth hidden from those who rejected or ignored Him and God's loving grace. "And He taught them many things by parables" (Mark 4:2). When we see the Apostles or other disciples not understanding, Jesus would clarify for them privately. "And when He was alone, those that were about Him with the twelve asked Him about the parable, and He said to them: "Unto you it is given to know the mystery of the Kingdom of God, but unto them that are without (outside of the Family of God), all these things are done in parables" (Mark 4:10-11). And then Christ would often proceed to explain the parable in specific detail so that His followers and believers would understand.

Even Christ's own disciples could not understand many of the parables, and required that it be explained to them. Sometimes, Christ would simply use another parable to explain the first, but often He would explain more specifically.

Why would Christ do that? Because God's perfect plan involves calling *many*, but choosing only a *few*. The *many* means that ***all*** are truly called, but *few* are truly chosen. (Matthew 22:14). Jesus made it very clear to those who followed and believed in Him: "You have not chosen Me, but I have chosen you" (John 15:16). In truth, God extends His call to every person who ever lives, but not every person chooses to listen, repent of sin, and trust in Jesus Christ as Savior. It is not enough for a person to live a good life. YOU MUST BE BORN AGAIN! Then, when you are born again of the Spirit, it is because God has chosen you as one of the *few*.

The Spiritual Truth here is that Jesus actually hid the meaning of His teachings from the many people of the world who were either rejecting Him or ignoring His message of love and salvation. The Lord's intention is to reveal the Spiritual Truth to His own: those people who are born-again of the Spirit by repentance of sin and faith in Jesus Christ as Lord. Jesus told His disciples, as He tells each of us who are His disciples today: "These things I have spoken to you in parables, but the time comes when I will not speak any more to you in parables, but I will show you plainly of the Father" (John 16:25). In other words, Jesus didn't always teach or speak to His own chosen Apostles plainly. But He did promise that the time would come when He would no longer use parables, but would be much more direct and clear, especially privately.

The general public did not understand Christ's teachings of parables. The Scribes and Pharisees of the religious Jewish order did not understand. On one occasion the religious hypocrites "perceived" that Christ was speaking about them, but they did not truly understand His meaning. In fact, Jesus Christ speaks in parables knowing fully well that many of the people who would hear His teachings would refuse to understand them. They would have "hardened hearts" toward Him and would refuse to listen and believe.

Even the Apostles did not always understand His parables. "And Jesus said to them (His disciples), how is it that you do not understand?" (Mark 8:21). "But they did not understand that saying, and were afraid to ask Him" (Mark 9:32). On another occasion Jesus said to His disciples: "Let these sayings sink down into your ears (let it soak into your understanding)...But they did not understand this saying, and it was hidden from them, and they did not perceive it; and were afraid to ask Him about it" (Luke 9:44, 45).

Jesus Christ taught His disciples (those people who believed in Him and followed Him) for over three years. They heard Him preach and teach many, many times, yet they had trouble understanding all that He taught, because of the parables. But, as the time for Christ's death, resurrection, and departure from them came near, He began to "open their eyes" and their understanding came in much more depth. When the Apostles and other followers began to mature Spiritually, Christ began to make His message and Spiritual Truth much clearer to them.

"These things His disciples did not understand at the first, but when Jesus was glorified (following His resurrection) then they remembered that these things were written about Him" (John 12:16).

At the last meeting Jesus had with His Apostles after His resurrection, He said to them: "These are the words which I spoke to you while I was yet with you, that all things must be fulfilled, which were written in the Law of Moses, in the prophets, and in the Psalms, concerning Me. Then, He opened their understanding, that they might understand the Scriptures" (Luke 24:44-45). Why did Jesus finally open their eyes? Because, it was Spiritually time for them to fully understand and go out to teach others these great Spiritual Truths.

"For whosoever has, to him shall be given, and he shall have more abundance; but whosoever has not, from him shall be taken away even what he has." Many people think this speaks of material or financial blessings. It does not speak of anything so worldly, but rather it speaks of Spiritual Truth and knowledge. Whoever truly has the Holy Spirit in his or her life will receive more and more Spiritual blessings and strength. Whoever does not have the life of the Spirit, will lose everything, including life itself, by perishing for all eternity in Hell and ultimately the Lake of Fire. (Revelation 20:14)

And so, how does all this pertain to us in this modern time? Actually, there is no better description of many of the organized churches of today than that found in Matthew 15:8-9, as Jesus speaks: "The people draw near to Me with their mouth, and honor Me with their lips, but their heart is far from Me. But in vain they worship Me, teaching for doctrines the commandments of men (of the world)." This refers to the false doctrines of today such as humanism, ritual religion for the sake of human pride, church organizational sanctity in place of true worship and dedication to the Lord.

To the chosen few, Jesus says: "Blessed are your eyes, for they see; and blessed are your ears, for they hear. For truly I say to you, that many prophets and righteous men have desired to see those things which you see, and have not seen them, and to hear those things which you hear, and have not heard them" (Matthew 13:16-17). This is spoken to the people who truly repent of sin and trust completely in Jesus Christ for all of life.

Following Christ's death and resurrection, and gathering at Pentecost (when the followers of Christ received God's Breath of the Holy Spirit upon them), men and women born of the Spirit were allowed to understand more clearly the things of the Spirit that Christ had been teaching all along while on the Earth. All of the prophecies of old, including the Revelation, are now being revealed to those who now are striving to learn more of God and His Spiritual Holiness.

The great Spiritual Truths and mysteries of the Kingdom will be clarified to those who diligently search and study God's Word in the Scriptures, while being earnest in their prayers for greater wisdom and knowledge of His Truth.

Many theologians, Bible scholars, and even pastors never truly understand the Scriptures and the things of the Spirit. Many people who call themselves "Christians" and are even members of local organized churches (often for the wrong reasons), do not understand the things of the Spirit, and are teaching and following the "commandments of men." Many people are drawing near to Christ with their lips, but their hearts are far from Him.

The only way to truly understand the things of the Spirit and the Holy Word of God is to be born again of the Spirit, and then follow Christ in daily life of Bible study and prayer, committing and submitting your life to the Lord Jesus Christ. "The natural man of this world does not receive and understand the things of the Spirit of God, for they are foolishness to him: neither can he know them, because Spiritual things are Spiritually discerned" (1 Corinthians 2:14).

So, it is a fact that you can only understand God's Word and Spiritual Truth, such as the Kingdom, when you are born of the Spirit, and diligently seek His Truth. When we get to the point in our Spiritual life that we are literally consumed with knowing God and His Truth more clearly, then we can truly understand what Christ has been teaching us all along. In fact, when we do see God's Spiritual Truth clearly, we are usually amazed that we didn't get it before. But, we were not able to understand certain things earlier in our life because we had not yet matured enough as a Spiritual child of God to really perceive and understand. As the very special preacher and teacher, Oswald Chambers, once put it: "Many people are not able to understand the things of the Spirit because the Son of Man has not yet risen in them."

The Lord does not always hide His Truth from His own child, but He does wait until we are ready in order to allow us the full understanding. Christ told His disciples: "I still have many things to say to you, but you cannot bear them now" (John 16:12). So, Christ really means to reveal His sacred Truth to us when we are ready in our life. And, in fact, the true evidence that we are becoming more mature in our Spiritual life is the fact that we do understand His Word, and His great mysteries of the Kingdom.

Jesus Christ is the greatest teacher who ever lived. He taught (and still teaches) in such a way that the learner is able to discover the truth of the information for self. The best teachers know that the very best and most meaningful learning takes place through self-discovery. Whenever the "light" comes on in the mind of a student, and he or she discovers the truth and the meaning, then true learning has taken place.

My earnest prayer for you is that "The Son of Man" will rise within you, and that you will be born of the Spirit, leading to your deep and abiding understanding of the Kingdom.

(Note: Chapter Eight of this writing)

THREE

The Kingdom

"From that time Jesus began to preach, and to say, Repent, for the Kingdom of Heaven is at hand." (Matthew 4:17)

Over the years I have had quite a few people ask me the question: "What is the difference between the *Kingdom of God* and the *Kingdom of Heaven*?" My answer to this question is usually as concise as I can make it, without diminishing the immense importance of this Spiritually-critical question. I have developed sermons over just this topic. I am even now writing this book on the topic. However, I don't pretend to have the all-inclusive and final answer, since I don't fool myself into thinking I have that much wisdom. I only know what I accept as absolute Truth by faith, from the teaching of my Lord Jesus Christ. Christ has allowed me to see the Spiritual Truth regarding the *Kingdom*, and it is my earnest desire to share it with you.

My short version of an answer to this profound question is: The difference between the Kingdom of God and the Kingdom of Heaven is like the difference between God the Father, God the Son, and God the Holy Spirit. Each has an individual function and effect, but exists as One God-Head that we refer to as the Holy Trinity. The Kingdom of God and the Kingdom of Heaven each has an individual function and effect, but exists as the One True Spiritual Kingdom. In fact, Jesus

Himself used the terms almost interchangeably and synonymously, although He did make some distinction as well.

First, let us consider the meaning of a *kingdom* and just why God chooses to use this term to describe His Spiritual existence. The dictionary defines a *kingdom* as being "a political or territorial unit ruled by a sovereign." It is also defined as "a country whose ruler is a king or queen." In the natural world, the term *kingdom* is used to specify the entire existence of either plants or animals in the world. Every living thing is either a member of the *plant kingdom* or *animal kingdom*, and falls under the science of *Biology*, which is the study of life.

So, God has chosen to present His entire Spiritual existence as being His *Kingdom*, with Himself serving as Sovereign Ruler. As difficult as it may be to understand and grasp, God's Kingdom includes more than the entire universe, with the vast expanse of the heavens and all of the galaxies, both known and unknown. After all, God actually created the universe itself, complete with all the stars, space matter, black holes, and everything else imaginable. God's physical creation is simply a part of His entire Spiritual Kingdom. God's Kingdom has existed for all eternity prior to His creation, exists now as He has brought it down to our Earth and presented it to every living human being, and will continue to exist for all eternity future. The major point being that God's Kingdom is Spiritual, and is not limited to the physical. He has simply chosen to use the term *Kingdom* to describe His Spiritual existence. Time, matter, the entire universe, all of earth and its contents, including all of humanity, all the hosts of Heaven, and everything created by God is a part of the Kingdom of God. All of creation, all of history, and all of existence will one day be absorbed into and made a part of the final Kingdom of God.

As the great theologian, C.I. Scofield, points out in his *Study Bible*, "the expression, 'the Kingdom of God', although used in many cases as synonymous with 'the Kingdom of Heaven', is to be distinguished from it in some instances." At times, we see the Kingdom of God viewed as everlasting and universal, being ruled by the Sovereign God over all things in the entire universe. In this sense, the Kingdom of God includes the Kingdom of Heaven. The Kingdom of God is also used to designate the Spiritual sphere of *Salvation*, which is entered only by the new birth of the Holy Spirit (John 3:5-7).

The Kingdom of Heaven is most often used in a more earthly reference, since it is the presentation of the Kingdom brought to this earth by Jesus Christ. It is considered to be the aspect of the Kingdom of God in which the true Church exists, made up of all born again believers and followers of Jesus Christ.

Since the Kingdom of Heaven is in the earthly realm of the universal Kingdom of God, the two have most things in common, being from the same source. In many contexts in God's Word, the two are interchangeable. Like the Kingdom of Heaven, the Kingdom of God is realized in the rule of God in this present age and will also be fulfilled in the future millennial kingdom ruled by Jesus Christ. It continues forever in its eternal state.

I have had people ask me the question: "If God is the King of His Kingdom, then why is Jesus Christ referred to as The King?" Well, that brings us to another Spiritual issue. Jesus Christ **is** God in the flesh, Who came down from His place in Heaven and presented the *Kingdom of God* to mankind, and making the *Kingdom of Heaven* available and accessible to each of us. Jesus Christ **is King**, just as Jesus Christ **is God**.

Christ clarified His sovereign position for us as He stated: "I and My Father are One" (John 10:30). He further asserts that, "If you had known Me, you should have known My Father also; and from now on, you know Him, and have seen Him" (John 14:7). Like so many of us, Philip, one of Christ's chosen Apostles, made the observation: "Lord, show us the Father, and it will be enough for us" (John 14:8). And Jesus clarified further: "Have I been such a long time with you, and yet you have not known Me, Philip? Anyone that has seen Me has seen the Father; and how can you say then, Show us the Father? Do you not believe that I am in the Father, and the Father is in Me? The words that I speak to you, I speak not of Myself; but the Father that dwells in Me, He does the works. Believe Me that I am in the Father, and the Father is in Me; or else believe Me for the very works that I do (miracles)" (John 14:9-11).

Perhaps the greatest Spiritual Truth of all is the fact that God the Father, God the Son (Jesus Christ), and God the Holy Spirit are each individual in their function and actions within the Kingdom of God, but yet are One and the Same in the true Spiritual sense. This concept is referred to as the Holy Trinity of God: God in Three Persons, and yet One Sovereign Ruler of all creation and of His Kingdom.

Although this may not be easy to understand during our life, it is one of the major Spiritual Truths that God expects His Spiritual children to accept by faith. He promises to make it all extremely clear to us when we are present with Him in eternal Heaven. As the sacred old hymn pronounces, "We'll understand it all by and by." The Truth is that God wants you and me to understand this great Truth now, and include it as part of our life in Him.

God's Kingdom or reign is a "process" and not simply an object or person. The Kingdom of God is the Spiritual existence and realm of God Almighty, and includes His Kingdom of Heaven, as well as His entire creation. In fact, God presents Himself to us as being "on His Throne" in His dwelling place, which is called *Heaven*. As the Psalmist declares, "Your throne, O God, is forever and ever: The scepter of your Kingdom is a right scepter" (Psalm 45:6). "God reigns over the heathen: God sits upon the throne of His holiness" (Psalm 47:8). The prophet Isaiah revealed his vision of God as Sovereign King as he declared, "I saw the Lord sitting upon a throne, high and lifted up, and His train filled the Temple" (Isaiah 6:1). The words of the Lord Jesus Christ further reveals: "I say unto you, do not swear at all; neither by Heaven; for it is God's Throne" (Matthew 5:34). "And he who swears by Heaven swears by God's Throne and by the One Who sits on it" (Matthew 23:22).

Now, there can also be a distinction between the Kingdom of God and the Kingdom of Heaven. While the Kingdom of God includes all of God's creation, as well as His Kingdom of Heaven, the Kingdom of Heaven is the reign of Jesus Christ in humanity during this present age, from the time of His birth until the time of His Second Coming.

The Kingdom of Heaven can also be referred to as "Christendom." Wherever the influence of Jesus Christ touches human beings is part of the Kingdom of Heaven. This present time prior to Christ's Second Coming to this earth is the time of the Kingdom of Heaven. This time in the history of the world is the time allowed by God for human beings to accept His loving Grace and His offer of eternal Salvation. Whenever a person repents of sin and trusts fully in Jesus Christ as Savior, he or she is born again of the Spirit and immediately becomes a part of the Kingdom of Heaven, and eternally, the Kingdom of God.

The Kingdom of Heaven is brought to this earth by Jesus Christ and made available to anyone who will repent of sin and trust in Him. The Kingdom of God takes in all of the Kingdom of Heaven as well as all of eternal existence.

God is King and Sovereign Ruler of His Kingdom, and Heaven is His Throne. What an exciting Truth. Jesus Christ is King of kings and Lord of lords and came to this Earth as God incarnate. What an exciting Truth. Jesus Christ came and fulfilled God's Kingdom purpose here on Earth by making the Kingdom of Heaven available to every living individual who will repent of sin and trust totally and completely in Jesus Christ as Lord, Savior, and King. What an exciting Truth!

The Old Testament Kingdom

"Your Throne, O God, is forever and ever" Psalm 45:6

In the beginning of our world, following God's creation of the human race, God established His Kingdom with mankind. God gave mankind the power of dominion over His creation and this entire Earth. "And God said, Let us make man in our image, after our likeness; and let them have dominion over the fish of the sea, and over the fowl of the air, and over the cattle, and over all the Earth, and over every creeping thing that creeps upon the Earth" (Genesis 1:26). Here we see that God gave the human race the authority over His Earthly Kingdom. However, God never gives His authority over His Spiritual Kingdom to any person, except the Person of Jesus Christ, His own Son Who is One and the Same in God Almighty.

We see here that God has established His "Earthly Kingdom" as a part of His Spiritual Kingdom. God's Earthly Kingdom includes all of His creation and was originally designed by God to allow mankind to rule over it. However, mankind proved to be sinful and disobedient to God, thereby losing the authority to rule over God's Kingdom here on Earth. When Adam and Eve sinned against God through their disobedience, they fell from the perfect grace of God and brought the entire human race down to a sinful state with them. From that point, Satan and his sin took over the authority of this physical world, but certainly not the Earthly Kingdom of God. God absolutely maintains power and authority over His Kingdom, both Spiritually and Physically. But God does allow Satan to exercise power within this physical world. In fact, we see that Satan even had the power to tempt the Lord Himself. In Matthew, Chapter 4, we see the Lord Jesus Christ coming out of a time of fasting and prayer in the wilderness. As Christ came out of the wilderness, Satan met Him and tried to influence Him into sin.

"Then was Jesus led up by the Spirit into the wilderness to be tempted (tested) by the devil. And when He had fasted forty days and forty nights, He was afterward hungry. And when the tempter came to Him, he said; 'If you are really the Son of God, command these stones to be made into bread.' But He answered and said; 'It is written, Man shall not live by bread alone, but by every word that proceeds out of the mouth of God.' Then the devil takes Him up into the holy city, and sets Him on a pinnacle of the temple, and says to Him; 'If you are the Son of God, cast yourself down; for it is written, He shall give His angels charge concerning you, and in their hands they will catch you and bring you up, lest at any time you should even dash your foot against a stone.' Jesus said to him; 'It is written again, You shall not put the Lord your God to the test.' Again, the devil takes Him up into an exceedingly high mountain, and shows Him all the kingdoms of the world, and the glory of them, and says to Him; 'All these things I will give to You, if You will fall down and worship me.' Then said Jesus to him; 'Get away from Me, Satan; for it is written, you shall worship the Lord your God, and Him only shall you serve.' Then, the devil left Him, and, behold, angels came and ministered unto Him" (Matthew 4:1-11).

We see here that Satan has the power to put people in places of authority in this world. Why, you ask: Because God has allowed that authority to be exercised by Satan at this time. God places each of us in the world and allows each of us to make decisions for ourselves as to who we will serve. God loves us and offers His perfect healing and salvation from the sin of the world, but He does not create us as robots. Our love for God must be voluntary and sincere.

We must love and serve God because we love and worship Him, not because God forces us to. After all, without sin and Satan, how could we even recognize God and His righteousness and holiness?

God's Word clarifies even further in Ephesians, Chapter 2: "And you has He made alive who were dead in trespasses and sins; in which in times past you walked according to the course of this world, according to the prince of the power of the air (Satan), the spirit that now works in the people of disobedience; among whom also we all had our manner of life in times past in the lusts of our flesh, fulfilling the desires of the flesh and of the mind, and were by nature the people of wrath, even as others. But God, Who is rich in mercy, for His great love with which He loved us, even when we were dead in sins, has made us alive together with Christ (by grace are you saved)."

And so, God saw that His creation, and the earthly and physical part of His Kingdom was being consumed by evil authority and living in sin. God determined that He would take the one truly faithful and righteous man in the world and establish a different form of authority over His earthly Kingdom. God appointed and directed Noah to prepare for a great flood that would take the life of all sinful people on the earth. God chose Noah's family of three sons, their wives, and Noah's wife to be saved from the flood and to re-populate the earth.

When God destroyed the earth's population with the great flood, He also determined to make a covenant with mankind for the remainder of history. God had made a covenant with Adam, which Adam broke with his sin. Now God would make a covenant with Noah and the new population of earth. The Noahic Covenant reaffirms the conditions of life of sinful man as the results of the Adamic Covenant, and then institutes the principle of human government to control the continuation of sin in the world. The elements of this Covenant include:

1. Man is made responsible to protect the sanctity of human life by organizing the orderly rule and authority over individual

people, including the death penalty for those who violate the orders. (Gen. 9:5-6; Romans 13:1-7)

2. God does not place any further curse on the Earth and mankind will not need to fear another universal flood that would destroy all the Earth. (Gen. 8:21; 9:11-16)
3. God confirms the order of nature for the remainder of history. (Gen. 8:22; 9:2)
4. The flesh of animals is added to man's diet and it can be assumed that mankind was a vegetarian prior to the great flood. (Gen. 9:3-4)
5. Noah places a curse on his own grandson, Canaan, for the sin of his father (Ham), and Canaan and his descendants would be servants and slaves to their relatives. (Gen. 9:25-26)
6. Another prophecy is declared that Shem (one of Noah's 3 sons) and his descendants will have a special relationship with God. C.I. Scofield, in his most revealing Study Bible Notes, points out that "all Divine revelation is through the Semitic race of people, and Jesus Christ, in the physical sense, descends from Shem." (Gen. 9:26-27)
7. Prophecy is also revealed that from Japheth will descend the "enlarged" races of people, which includes Europeans, Russians, and other Gentiles (Gen. 9:27). Government, science, and art in the broadest sense, have come from the Japhetic races.

In fact, the history of our world bears the indisputable record of the fulfillment of these declarations found in Genesis regarding the three sons of Noah and their descendants. Descending from Ham are the races of people primarily from Africa, including Egypt. Descending from Shem are the races of people primarily from Asia, including Israel and Arabia, as well as China and other Asian areas. Descending from Japheth are the races of people primarily from Europe, including Russia, Iran, and Iraq.

It was through the blessings God showed to Shem and his descendants that we find the physical lineage of the Messiah: The

Lord Jesus Christ. Of course, Christ's true lineage is Spiritual and is part of God Almighty. Because of this special blessing to Shem and his descendants, God established His earthly Kingdom within the nation of Israel, which are the descendants of Abraham.

The call of Abraham by God involved the creation of a distinctive people through whom the great purposes of God toward the human race would be fulfilled. Through Abraham and his descendants (the Nation of Israel) God would bring about His sacred and holy commandments and laws. This would constitute God's establishment of His world-wide Kingdom here on Earth, through the most important descendant of all: Jesus Christ. Christ was the fulfillment of God's Kingdom when He came to Earth and sacrificed Himself for the sins of the world, and Christ will be the perfect future fulfillment of God's Eternal Kingdom when He returns to Earth in power and great glory to take His rightful and imminent place as the King of all kings and Lord of all lords. In future eternity, Jesus Christ will reign over the eternal Kingdom of God.

The history of God's establishment and rule over His Divine Kingdom here on Earth is as follows:

1. God established His laws for His Kingdom under Moses, as He used Moses to bring His chosen people out of slavery in Egypt and into His chosen role for them as His people chosen to administer His earthly Kingdom. (Ex. 19:3-7; Ex. 3:1-10; Ex. 24:12)
2. God administered His Kingdom through His chosen leaders and judges. (Joshua 1:1-5; Judges 2:16-18)
3. God also administered His Kingdom through His chosen earthly kings. (1 Samuel 10:1, 24; 1 Samuel 16:1-13; 1 Kings 9:1-5)
4. God used Babylon as His agent of judgment against Israel for their sins of idolatry and rebellion against Him. Under the reign of King Nebuchadnezzar II, the Babylonian Empire spread throughout the Middle East. The Babylonians first took control of Judah and held the brightest young men from each

city in Judah captive, including Daniel, Hananiah (Shadrach), Mishael (Meshach), and Azariah (Abednego). Following a revolt by Judah, with the help of Egypt, Nebuchadnezzar went to quell the rebellion and while doing so, laid siege to Jerusalem, taking God's people captive and essentially ending the Old Testament Kingdom as God had established it. The Jews were held in captivity and exile for 70 years. (Ezekiel 21:25-27; Jeremiah 27:6-8; Daniel 2:36-38; and the books of 2 Chronicles and 2 Kings)

Some of the Old Testament prophets during the time of the Babylonian captivity included Jeremiah, one of the prophets during the time leading up to the fall of Jerusalem and the exile. Ezekiel and Daniel were the Old Testament books written while the Jews were in exile. The book of Ezra deals with the return of the Jews as God promised through the prophets Jeremiah and Isaiah. The book of Nehemiah also deals with the return of the Jews to their homeland and the rebuilding of Jerusalem after the exile was over.

The Babylonian captivity had a most significant impact on the Nation of Israel when it was able to return home. Israel as a nation would never again be corrupted by the idolatry and worship of false gods like the nations surrounding them. The Jews returned to Israel and rebuilt the temple, igniting a revival among the people of Israel. The nation would once again return to God as their strength and deliverer. As you may recall from study of history, Israel became a true Nation in 1948 when the Jewish people began to return to their homeland, according to God's prophecy and promise.

Also noteworthy is the fulfillment of the promise of God through the prophet Jeremiah of God's judgment on the Babylonians for their sins. The Babylonian Empire fell to the armies of Persia in 539 B.C., once again proving God's promises to always be true.

The historical account of God's earthly Kingdom established with His chosen people of Israel fully demonstrates God's faithfulness to His people, His judgment of sin, and the certainty of His promises.

FIVE

The New Testament Kingdom

"In those days came John the Baptist, preaching in the wilderness of Judea, and saying, Repent; for the Kingdom of Heaven is at hand." (Matthew 3:1-2)

According to the C.I. Scofield Study Bible, the expression "kingdom of heaven" literally means "out of the heavens", and refers to the power, authority, and rule of the heavens. In other words, it refers to the rule of God of Heaven over the Earth and, in the pure sense, the reign of Jesus Christ as King of kings and Lord of lords.

As used by John the Baptist in his ministry on Earth, the term "kingdom of heaven" is used to refer to Jesus Christ as the King and ruler over the purpose and will of God toward all of mankind. Jesus Christ came to Earth from His position in God on the true Throne of the Kingdom of God in Heaven. Christ came for the express purpose of establishing God's Kingdom on Earth and perfectly fulfilling all of God's laws established in history past. Christ came to fulfill the law of God, and to give His life as the ultimate sacrifice for the sins of the whole world, including the sins of every individual who would ever live on this Earth. By giving His life on the Cross, Christ did indeed fulfill the entire Law of God in every respect and in every specific point (See Matthew 5:17). That is why God's Law of the

Old Testament was fulfilled and reinforced by Christ's Law of the New Testament. No longer do people have to sacrifice the blood of animals in order to repent of sin and be forgiven and cleansed. It is now necessary only to repent of sin and place faith and trust in Jesus Christ as the means by which you can be forgiven and inherit eternal life. Jesus Christ is the only blood sacrifice necessary for salvation and eternal life.

The entire future restoration and administration of God's Kingdom is placed in the person of Jesus Christ. The Kingdom of God has been the Spiritual existence of God for all eternity past and God's Kingdom of Heaven has always, and will always be established for His own family. Would you like to be a part of the Kingdom of God and a citizen of the Kingdom of Heaven? You can be. You must first realize and admit that you are a sinner, having violated God's holiness and righteousness by being disobedient to Him in your life. You must earnestly and sincerely repent of your sins and go to God in prayer, in the Holy Name of Jesus Christ as your Lord and King. When you repent of sin and trust by faith in Christ Jesus as Lord, you are born again of the Spirit and become a member of God's family, being born into the Kingdom of Heaven by the holy and righteous sacrifice of Jesus Christ, with Christ serving as your Mediator to God Almighty.

The New Testament Kingdom of Heaven was described by the prophets and was to be established under the lineage of King David. David's heir was to be born of a virgin, and being truly physical man, but also born of God, being called "Immanuel," "The mighty God, the everlasting Father, the Prince of Peace" (Isaiah 7:13-14; 9:6-7; 11:1; Jeremiah 23:5; Ezekiel 34:23; 37:24; Hosea 4:3-5).

The New Testament Kingdom of Heaven was to be a part of the dwelling place and Spirit of God in its origin, principle, and authority, but set up on the Earth, with Jerusalem as the capital (Daniel 2:34-35, 44-45; Isaiah 2:2-4; 4:3; 24:23; 33:20; 62:1-7; Jeremiah 23:5; 31:38-40; Joel 3:1; 16-17).

The New Testament Kingdom of Heaven was to be established over re-gathered, restored, and converted Israel, and is then to become universal, including all people of the Earth (Psalm 2:6-8; 22:1-31; 24:1-10; Isaiah 1:2-3; 11:1, 10-13; 60:12; Jeremiah 23:5-8; 30:7-11; Ezekiel 20:33-44; 37:21-25; Zechariah 9:10; 14:16-19). The establishment of Israel as a nation in 1948, and the subsequent re-gathering of the Jewish people to their homeland is the evidence of truth in this sacred prophecy. Also, the offering of true access to the Kingdom to all the people of the world was to be established by Jesus Christ Himself, through the testimony of His Apostles (Acts 13:47-48; 28:28; Romans 1:16; 2:9-10; 11:11).

Then, we see the prophecy of the future Kingdom of Heaven to be established beyond this Earth and into God's eternal purpose for His own people. This Spiritual aspect of the Kingdom will be in place following the Second Advent of the Lord Jesus Christ in "power and great glory." The characteristics of the New Kingdom of Heaven under Jesus Christ are to be righteousness and peace. The meek, not the proud, will inherit the Earth; longevity will be greatly increased; the knowledge of the Lord will be universal; the savage ferocity of beasts will be removed; absolute equity will be enforced; and open sin will be dealt with by instant judgment; a large number of Earth's inhabitants will be saved (Psalm 2:9; Isaiah 11:4, 6-9; 26:9; 65:20; Zechariah 14:16-21). Then, the New Testament Scripture of Revelation 20:1-5 adds another very significant detail to the characteristics of the New Kingdom of Heaven: Satan will be removed from the scene. This portion of the New Kingdom will take place for 1,000 years during the "millennial reign of Jesus Christ" here on Earth.

The future establishment of the New Kingdom on Earth with Christ reigning as King will be brought about by the mighty power of Christ, and not the friendly persuasion He used during His earthly ministry and the Age of the Church between His sacrifice on the Cross and His Second Coming back to Earth. Just prior to this time of the Kingdom, Christ will bring judgment upon the Gentile world powers that have rejected Him and served Satan (Psalm 2:4-9; Isaiah 9:7; Daniel 2:35, 44-45; 7:26-27; Zechariah 14:1-19; 6:11). This restoration of the Nation of Israel and the establishment of the Kingdom of Heaven here on Earth will be related directly to the Second Coming of the Lord Jesus Christ in power and great glory, which is yet in the future (Deuteronomy 30:3-5; Psalm 2:1-9; Zechariah 14:4).

The Lord Jesus Christ speaks of His Kingdom and those who followed Him faithfully as His chosen Apostles. Jesus says: "Truly I say to you that you who will follow Me, in the *regeneration*, when the Son of man will sit on the throne of His glory, you also shall sit upon twelve thrones, judging the twelve tribes of Israel (Matthew 19:28). Christ's statement here shows that the future Kingdom of Heaven will also include similar administration under the authority of judges.

In the following verse of Scripture (Matthew 19:29), Christ includes those of us who have repented of sin and trusted in Him as Lord and King, following Him during our lives on this Earth. Christ says: "And every one that has forsaken houses, or brothers, or sisters, or father, or mother, or wife, or children, or lands, for my Name's sake, will receive a hundredfold, and will inherit everlasting life."

The word *regeneration* appears only one other time in the New Testament (Titus 3:5), and refers to the new birth of the Christian in the Spirit. In Matthew 19:28, the word refers to the re-creation of the social order and renewal of the Earth when the Kingdom comes with Christ at His Second Coming (Isaiah 11:6-9; Romans 8:19-23; Acts 3:21; 1 Corinthians 15:24). The Lord's prediction in Matthew 19:28 shows how the promise of Isaiah 1:26 will be fulfilled when the Kingdom is set up. The Kingdom future will be administered over Israel through the Apostles, according to the ancient judges (Judges 2:18).

And so, we see that the Kingdom of Heaven as established by God in the Old Testament is brought into the New Testament by Jesus Christ and developed in a sequential order:

1. The promise of the Kingdom to David and his lineage (his "seed"), and described by the prophets of old, enters into the New Testament unchanged (Luke 1:31-33). The King was born in Bethlehem (Matthew 2:1 and Micah 5:2), and was born of a virgin (Matthew 1:18-25 and Isaiah 7:14).

2. The Kingdom was announced as being "at hand" by the prophet John the Baptist, the forerunner of Christ (Matthew 4:17). The Kingdom was also announced by Christ Himself as King, and by the Twelve Apostles.
3. The Kingdom was rejected by the Jewish people of Israel, even as God's "chosen people." The Jews rejected Christ and the Kingdom both morally and officially (Matthew 11:20; 21:42-43), and "crowned" Christ as King only in a sadistic and hateful manner: with a crown of thorns, prior to crucifying Him on a cruel cross.
4. Christ, in anticipation of His rejection and crucifixion, revealed His "mysteries" of the Kingdom of Heaven, to be fulfilled in the interval between His rejection and death, and His return to Earth in power and great glory (Matthew 13:1-50).
5. The Lord announced His purpose to "build", or establish His Church during the interval between His life and death, His resurrection, and His return to Earth. The Church of the Body of Christ is another great "mystery" which is now being fulfilled in this present age, along with the "mysteries of the Kingdom of Heaven" (Matthew 16:18; Ephesians 3:9-11). Therefore, the "mysteries of the Kingdom of Heaven" and the "mystery of the Church" occupy the same period of time: this present age we now live in, which began with the birth of Jesus Christ, His death on the Cross, His resurrection, His ascension back to Heaven, and will culminate with His return to the Earth at His Second Advent.
6. The "mysteries of the Kingdom" will be brought to an end by the "harvest" Christ speaks of in Matthew 13:39-43, 49-50. First, Christ will take His Church to be with Him prior to His Second Return to Earth (The Rapture: 1 Thessl 4:13-17).
7. Then Christ will come to the Earth in "power and great glory" to put an end to the evil of Satan and his armies of nations.
8. Upon His return, the King will restore the royal reign of King David in a truly Spiritual sense, as He takes His rightful place

on the throne of the Kingdom. Christ will re-gather dispersed Israel, and will establish His power and rule over the entire Earth, where He will reign for 1,000 years (Matthew 24:27-30; Acts 15:14-17; Revelation 20:1-10).

9. The Kingdom of Heaven, established under "David's Divine Son, will serve to restore the Divine authority in the Earth, which can be regarded as a sort of "physical part" of the great Kingdom of God (Matthew 3:2; 6:33).

As a note: The Kingdom Age of 1,000 years with Christ reigning here on Earth, constitutes the "Seventh Dispensation" of Revelation 20:4. When Christ defeats the last enemy, death, then He will deliver up the Kingdom to "God, even the Father" so that God as the Triune God (God the Father, God the Son, and God the Holy Spirit) "may be all in all" (1 Corinthians 15:24-28). The eternal Throne of the Kingdom is known as the "Throne of God and of the Lamb" (Revelation 22:1).

To further clarify, C.I. Scofield points out that, "the Kingdom of God, although used in many cases as synonymous with the Kingdom of Heaven, is to be distinguished from it in some instances. The Kingdom of God is at times viewed as everlasting and universal, and is considered the rule of sovereign God over all creatures and things. In this sense the Kingdom of God includes the Kingdom of Heaven." (Matthew 3:2; Psalm 103:19; Daniel 4:3).

Most critically, the Kingdom of God is also used to designate the entire inclusion of those people who have been "saved" from the punishment of hell and the eventual Lake of Fire, and have had their names written in the *Lamb's Book of Life*, thus securing their place in Heaven for all eternity. This "sphere of salvation" includes the Old Testament saints who were included by faith in God and belief in the future of Jesus Christ as the Messiah, as well as the New Testament saints who have been redeemed by the blood of Christ through their repentance of sin and total faith in Christ, being born again of the Spirit (John 3:5-7). The Old Testament saints were brought into the family of God by their faith in Him. Their faith in God will save them. The New Testament saints are brought into the Church, the blessed Bride of Christ, containing all of those who have trusted by faith in Christ as their sacrifice and have been cleansed of their sins by Christ. And so, the Church is a blessed part of the Kingdom of Heaven, and is eternally a part of the Kingdom of God.

The Kingdom of Heaven, as we have it presented to us today by God's Word, is in the earthly sphere of the universal Kingdom of God, and the two have many things in common. In some contexts the terms are interchangeable, as long as the distinguishing features can also be understood.

Like the Kingdom of Heaven, the Kingdom of God is present with us in the rule of God in the present age, and will also be fulfilled in the future millennial Kingdom. It will continue forever in the eternal state (Daniel 4:3).

SIX

Mysteries of God

"For truly I say unto you that many prophets and righteous men have desired to see those things which you see, and have not seen them; and to hear those things which you hear, and have not heard them." (Matthew 13:17)

A "mystery" in Scripture is a previously hidden truth that is divinely revealed in the time frame of God. Perhaps one of the greatest mysteries of God is the interval of time between the birth of the Lord Jesus Christ (First Advent) and the return of the Lord Jesus Christ to Earth in power and great glory (Second Advent). (Matthew 13:17, 35; 1 Peter 1:10-12).

There are several "great mysteries" included during this interval of time, and can be considered to be a part of the "mysteries of the Kingdom of Heaven" (Matthew 13:3-50).

A. <u>Christ As God:</u> A great mystery God has revealed to His children in His Word is the "the mystery of God, even Christ." It is simply not possible in human terms to fully describe the nature and identity of God. Our finite human minds cannot even begin to conceive of the Divine Spiritual nature of God: His omnipotence, His omniscience, and His omnipresence. God is all-powerful, all-knowing, and ever-present. After all, by definition, a mystery is a concept that is not entirely revealed. There is an element to any mystery that will remain unknown to human beings. But, the great Truth of God is that He knows absolutely everything, He is in total and absolute control over everything, and He is present everywhere at the same time. What a phenomenal mystery to mankind!

To extend and expound on this mystery even further, Jesus Christ was born as a human baby to a young woman who had never known a man sexually. Now, that in itself is a human impossibility. It is simply not humanly possible for a child to be conceived in a mother's womb without the fertilization of the male seed. But, the greatest mystery of our world is the conception and birth of Jesus Christ, having been conceived by the Holy Spirit of God inside the womb of a virgin woman, and brought into this world in human form. How do we explain that? Well, we don't explain it any further than the information God gives us. We are asked to accept this great mystery by faith. But, whenever we do accept it as absolute fact and truth, then we are given access to the Kingdom of God.

Keep in mind that the simple belief that Jesus Christ was born of a virgin woman and was born into this world as "God in the Flesh," does not in itself give one eternal life and new birth of the Spirit. We each must confess and repent of our sins, then trusting by faith in the power of Jesus Christ to be our Lord and Savior. Then we can have our Spiritual birth and can then proceed with our intimate understanding of God's great mysteries, including the fact that Jesus Christ was God in human flesh and lived on this earth, living His life perfectly free from any sin, and sacrificing Himself on a cruel cross so that we might be cleansed of our sins and saved from eternal suffering in Hell and the Lake of Fire

As God's great Truth tells us: "God was in Christ, reconciling the world unto Himself.....For He has made Him Who knew no sin, to be sin for us; so that we might be made the righteousness of God in Him." (2 Corinthians 5:17-21)

The mystery of God, even Christ is this: That Jesus Christ is the incarnate fullness of the Godhead embodied in human form, and in Whom all of the Divine wisdom for mankind is held. As we see in 1 Corinthians 2:5-7: "your faith should not stand in the wisdom of men, but in the power of God. However, we speak wisdom among them that are perfect; yet not the wisdom of this world, nor of the princes of this world, that come to nothing; but we speak the wisdom of God in a mystery, even the hidden wisdom, which God ordained before the world unto our glory." This mystery is what the Holy Spirit of God teaches God's children who have been born again of the Spirit. And, in Colossians, Chapter 2, we see clarification for those who are born again of the Spirit: "that their hearts might be comforted, being knit together in love and unto all riches of the full assurance of understanding, to the acknowledgement of the mystery of God, and the Father, and of Christ, in Whom are hidden all the treasures of wisdom and knowledge. For in Him (Jesus Christ) dwells all the fullness of the Godhead bodily."

The "mystery of God" is Jesus Christ, as being God in the Flesh and having all of the fullness of the Godhead (which consists of God the Father, God the Son, and God the Holy Spirit). Jesus Christ was, and is, the embodiment of this Holy Trinity of God. All of the Divine wisdom and knowledge for the redemption, reconciliation, and salvation of all mankind lies within Jesus Christ. That is why it is absolutely critical that each person repents of sin and places his or her complete trust and faith in Jesus Christ: In order to receive a new birth of the Spirit, and a new life in Heaven for all eternity.

B. The Indwelling Christ: Another great mystery of the Kingdom is the mystery of the "in-living Christ," also referred to as "the indwelling Christ." From the very beginning of His ministry and teaching here on Earth, Jesus Christ spoke of Himself being **"in God"** and God being **"in Him."** In this regard, Jesus is

> speaking in the Spiritual sense. Christ points out that "I and My Father are one" (John 10:30). In fact, when Christ pointed out to His Apostles that they should know God the Father since they have known Him, the Apostle Philip said, "Lord, show us the Father, and it will be sufficient." Jesus said to him, "Have I been with you such a long time, and yet you have not really known Me, Philip? He that has seen Me has seen the Father; and how can you say, 'show us the Father?' Don't you believe that I am in the Father, and the Father is in Me? Believe Me when I tell you that I am in the Father, and the Father is in Me, or else believe Me because of the works that I do." (John 14:7-12). Spiritually, Jesus Christ and God is one and the same. God is Spiritually **in** Jesus Christ, and Christ is **in** God, meaning that the two are the same in their existence and Spiritual "Person." In addition, the Holy Spirit of God is also the same as God the Father and Jesus Christ. These three Divine Persons exist as One Holy Trinity, being **in** each other as One in Spirit.

The profound truth of God also, is that God will Spiritually come into you and me whenever we are "born again of the Spirit" by our repentance of sin and faith and trust in Jesus Christ as our Lord and Savior. The term "in" literally means "indwelling" the Spirit and Soul of the person who is born of the Spirit. The "in-living Christ" literally comes into the life of the regenerated person Spiritually, indwelling the person and making the person a new creation.

In the Scripture Gospel of John, in Chapter 17, the Lord Jesus Christ prays an intercessory prayer on behalf of His Apostles as well as all other people who come to believe and trust in Him for salvation. "As You (God the Father) have sent Me into the world, even so have I also sent them into the world. And for their sakes I sanctify Myself, so that they also might be sanctified through the Truth. I do not pray only for these (the chosen Apostles), but for them also who will believe on Me through their word; so that they all may be one, as You, Father, are in Me, and I in You, that they also may be one in Us; so that the world may believe that You have sent Me. And the glory which You gave Me I have given to them, so that they may be one, even as We are one: I in them, and You in Me, that they may be made perfect in one; and that the world may know that You have sent Me, and have loved them, just as You have loved Me." (John 17:18-23).

So, whenever I repented of my sin and trusted completely in Jesus Christ as Lord of my life, God gave me a completely new life in the Spirit. He Spiritually "Baptized" me with His Holy Spirit, meaning that God took away my old life of sin and replaced it with His new life of Spirit. God's Holy Spirit literally came in to indwell me, controlling my conscience and my Spiritual existence. The "in-living Christ" is truly the Holy Spirit living in me now, and for all eternity to come. Whenever I was born again of the Spirit, the Holy Spirit Himself began to "bear witness" with my Spirit, that I am a child of God (Romans 8:16).

The Apostle Paul helps to clarify this great mystery further in his writing to the Christians at Rome (Romans 8:8-11): "So, then, they that are in the flesh cannot please God. But you are not in the flesh but in the Spirit, if indeed the Spirit of God dwells in you. Now if any person does not have the Spirit of Christ, that person does not belong to Christ. And if Christ is in you, the body is dead because of sin, but the Spirit is life because of righteousness. But if the Spirit of Him that raised up Jesus from the dead dwells in you, he that raised up Christ from the dead will also give life to your mortal bodies by His Spirit that dwells in you." In other words, no one can please God in the flesh and within this physical world context. The only way to truly please God is to repent of sin and trust totally by faith in Jesus Christ as the Lord of your life. If Christ is not Lord of your life, then you don't belong to Christ, and the Spirit of God does not dwell, or live, in you. In truth, if Christ is in you, then your old sinful will of the flesh and this world is dead, and is replaced with the Holy Spirit of God, which is the Holy Spirit of Christ, and is in you to give you your new life of the Spirit.

Paul gives us a great testimony with his exemplary life when he says, "I am crucified with Christ: nevertheless I live; yet it is not me, but Christ living in me; and the life which I now live in the flesh I live by the faith of the Son of God, Who loved me and gave Himself for me" (Galatians 2:20).

Paul also summarizes this great mystery for us as he reminds us that he was especially chosen by God to be a minister of God's Word. Paul tells us, "Even the mystery which has been hidden from ages and from generations, but now is made manifest (is revealed) to His saints, to whom God would make known what is the riches of the glory of this mystery among Gentiles, which is ***Christ in you, the hope of glory***" (Colossians 1:26-27).

C. The Church: The mystery of the New Testament Church is one of the great mysteries that had been hidden from the Old Testament people. The New Testament Church is the Body of Christ and is made up of those people who earnestly repent of sin and trust fully in Jesus Christ as Lord. The New Testament Church is being "built" during this present time and will only end when the last person comes to the new birth of the Spirit, and becomes the final member of the Body of Christ. The true Church is made up of both Jews and Gentiles, since there are many Jews who have fully believed and trusted in Jesus Christ. Many Jews remain unbelieving and rejecting, but many have been born again by their faith in Christ. These Jews, along with the saved Gentiles make up the true Church as one body in Christ. (Ephesians 3:1-12; Romans 16:25; Ephesians 6:19; Colossians 4:3).

D. The Blindness of Israel: One of the mysteries hidden from the Old Testament prophets and revealed by Christ to His disciples, or true followers, is the mystery of the "blindness" of Israel during this age

> (Romans 11:25). The Apostle Paul is used by the Lord to help clarify this mystery for us. Paul writes: "For I would not have you be ignorant of this mystery, brothers and sisters in Christ, lest you should be thinking you are wiser than you really are in your conceits: that blindness in part is happened to Israel, until the fullness of the Gentiles are come in." Now just what does Paul mean by this? Well, the "fullness of the Gentiles" is the completion of the sovereign purpose of God during this age to call out chosen people from among the Gentile nations of the world. These people will be called and will heed God's call to repent and trust by faith in Jesus Christ as Lord. These people will be witnesses throughout the world for the sake of Jesus Christ and the salvation He offers. These will be people who are living in Christ's Name, serving and glorifying God through faith in Jesus Christ. These are truly the people who will be included in the True Church, which is the Spiritual Body of Christ. This interval of time and full completion of the Gentile people who will be a part of the Body of Christ is often referred to as "The Church Age", and was not revealed to the Old Testament prophets.

This mystery is further clarified when we realize that there will be one last and final person who has been "called" by God and chooses to surrender totally to Jesus Christ, who is born again of the Spirit and completes the Church in full.

This final person will complete the "fullness of the Gentiles" and the Church itself will be complete. When this occurs, Jesus Christ will call His Church, or His Body, to come to be with Him for all eternity. As we see in 1 Thessalonians 4:13-18, "the Lord Himself shall descend from Heaven with a shout, with the voice of the archangel, and with the trump of God; and the dead in Christ shall rise first; Then we who are alive and remain (on this Earth) shall be caught up together with them in the clouds, to meet the Lord in the air: and so shall we ever be with the Lord." This glorious event is referred to as the *Rapture*, a term most suitable to describe this sacred and awesome event. (Ephesians 1:22-23; Acts 15:14; 1 Corinthians 12:12-13; Ephesians 4:11-13)

Also, please note that the "fullness of the Gentiles" should not be confused with the "times of the Gentiles" noted in Luke 21:24. The "times of the Gentiles" refers to the period of time that Israel was held captive by the Gentiles of Babylon under King Nebuchadnezzar. The "fullness of the Gentiles" refers to the completion of the Church as the Body of Christ.

E. <u>The Translation of the Church:</u> Another of the great "mysteries of the Kingdom" is the mystery of the translation of the living saints at the end of this age (1 Corinthians 15:51-52; 1 Thess. 4:13-17). We discussed this mystery briefly in the paragraph above, referring to the instant that Jesus Christ calls His Body, the True Church, to be with Him. In that moment, "in the twinkling of an eye", the living saints who are born again of the Spirit and are in Christ Jesus will be changed with the Spiritual gift of a "transfigured" or transformed body. This will be a perfect body in the image of Jesus Christ and the body He received at His resurrection. In this new body, the true Christian will have no more sorrow or pain, but will be eternally in peace and comfort in the Lord. As we saw in 1 Thessalonians 4, those who have already died their physical death will receive their transfigured bodies first and will rise to meet the Lord. Then, those who remain alive will be changed into their new bodies and will follow to meet the Lord. This mystery is made clear to us through God's Word, just as the Holy Spirit of God revealed it to the Apostle Paul to write it down.

F. <u>The Revelation of Iniquity:</u> Another of the great mysteries of God is the mystery of *iniquity.* Iniquity is wickedness, or gross immorality. In short, iniquity is sin. It is the manifestation of evil in the life of the person committing iniquity. Every person born into this world is born into a life of iniquity. There is inherent evil and sin present in every life due to the presence of Satan, who is the author of evil and sin.

The working of the mystery of iniquity began with Satan's influence upon Eve and then Adam, as they were deceived into believing Satan and his lies, just as so many people are to this day. Part of the mystery of iniquity is that God allows Satan to use his influence and even power in this physical world to go about deceiving and influencing people to sin and maintain iniquity in their lives.

But, God has made provision for the restraint of total evil in the world by the power of His Holy Spirit Who is present in this world today to act as a restraint against Satan's evil in the lives of God's children (those born again of the Spirit).

In fact, the role of the Holy Spirit in our world has several facets. First of all, He is here to convict people of sin. The best restraint against a person being evil in life is a healthy and active conscience. The Holy Spirit works in the mind and conscience of a person and brings the person under guilty conviction of committing sin, causing the person to regret sin that he or she has committed, while avoiding committing many sins of evil altogether.

The Holy Spirit also works to lead a person to repentance of sin and provides the faith for the person to trust in Jesus Christ as Lord and Savior. In other words, it is the Holy Spirit that leads a person to be born again of the Spirit. Then, whenever the person is born of the Spirit, his or her Spirit bears witness with the Holy Spirit that he or she is a true child of God.

Whenever a person becomes a true child of God, the Holy Spirit then provides certain and absolute Spiritual protection from Satan and his evil power. Satan may continue to try to influence the physical life of the true Christian, but he has no power whatsoever over the Holy Spirit of God. While the Holy Spirit does not restrain evil altogether in the world, He does give absolute protection for the Spirit of the true, born-again child of God. This certain protection comes in Spiritual form. Satan has no power to attack the Spirit of the true Christian. While evil in this world can certainly act to kill anyone physically, it can never kill the Spirit. The person born of the Spirit possesses absolute eternal life. Upon physical death, I will be absent from my physical body, but I will be immediately present with the Lord in my Spirit and Soul. My physical death is in the Sovereign Will of God and will take place whenever God has determined that I should be with Him for eternity future. The point is: physical death has no dominion over the true, born-again child of God. Spiritual life is eternal. Following the time of the Church in the world, beginning with the First Advent of Christ and ending with Christ's taking of His Church out of the world (The Rapture), the Holy Spirit will be "taken out of the way" and evil will be allowed to take greater control of the world. This time of future history is known as the Tribulation and brings the final seven years of world history.

Keep in mind that Jesus Christ is going to call His own Church to be with Him prior to the evil Tribulation time led by Satan and his Antichrist and False Prophet. Those people who have been born again of the Spirit are the very ones who are a member of the True Church and the Body of Christ. Any who have died prior to this event (known to us as the Rapture) will rise first to meet the Lord, and those who remain alive will go to meet Him in the air. "And so shall we ever be with the Lord." (1 Thessalonians 4:13-18)

During the Church Age, the Holy Spirit worked through the Church, in the lives of those born again of the Spirit. With the Church taken from the earth, the Holy Spirit will not function as the restraint against evil that He once was.

Immediately following the Rapture of the Church by the Lord Jesus Christ, the Holy Spirit will be taken out of the way of restraining evil. Notice that the Holy Spirit will not be "taken away" but will be "taken out of the way". He will still be very active in the world, convicting those left behind at the Rapture that they still have a chance to repent and trust in Christ. There will still be an opportunity for people to be saved and born again during the evil of the Tribulation. The Holy Spirit will continue to influence, but will not be the restraint He was during the Church Age. (Study 2 Thessalonians 2:1-12)

With the Church gone and the restraint of the Holy Spirit taken out of the way, the evil one (Satan), referred to as "the man of sin" and "the son of perdition" will be allowed to display and produce the evil only Satan can bring about.

But, praise be to God, the return of Christ to this earth at His Second Advent will put an end to Satan and the evil he produces. Christ will overthrow the "man of sin" and will establish His millennial Kingdom here on earth for 1,000 years. (Refer to 2 Thess. 2:8-10 and Revelation 19:11 through 20:6)

> **G. The Bride of Christ:** An additional mystery of the Kingdom is the mystery of the true Church as the "Bride of Christ." (Ephesians 5:22-32). The Apostle Paul writes to us in his letter to the Church at Ephesus and uses the analogy of the husband and his relationship to the wife in a holy marriage. Paul compares the relationship of a wife to her husband to the relationship the Christian should have to Jesus Christ, in the Spiritual sense. Note: "Wives, submit yourselves to your own husbands, as unto the Lord." Paul goes on to compare Christ, as head of His Church, to the husband, as head of the wife. The "body" refers to the complete sphere of saved souls, having been born again of the Spirit, and living in one accord, in service and dedication to Jesus Christ. Just as the Church is subject to Christ, let wives be subject to their husbands.

Just as husbands should love their wives, Christ loves His Church, and gave Himself for it. Christ sanctifies and cleanses His Church as the husband and wife should be clean and faithful and loving to each other. Christ cleanses His Church to the point that He can "present it to Himself a glorious Church, not having spot, or wrinkle, or any such thing; but that it should be holy and without blemish." So should men love their wives just as their own bodies, just as Christ loves His Church as part of Himself. Paul adds that "we are members of His Body, of His flesh, and of His bones." In verse 32 of Ephesians 5, Paul points out that "this is a great mystery, but I speak concerning Christ and the Church."

In fact, God's Word further uses the analogy of a marriage relationship between Jesus Christ and His Church in The Revelation to John. In Revelation 19:7-9, the angel of the Lord speaks to John: "Let us be glad and rejoice, and give honor to Him; for the marriage of the Lamb is come and His wife has made herself ready. And to her was granted that she should be arrayed in fine linen, clean and white; for the fine linen is the righteousness of saints. And he said unto me, Write, Blessed are they who are called unto the marriage supper of the Lamb. And he said unto me, These are the true sayings of God." The "Marriage Supper of the Lamb" is the great event in Heaven where Jesus Christ takes His true Church, which is Spiritually part of His Body, and sanctifies and identifies it forever as being loved and cared for by Him for all eternity to come.

H. <u>The Reconciliation of Mankind:</u> An additional mystery we find in God's Word is the mystery of the processes by which original likeness with God can be restored to mankind. As we have seen in God's original creation of human beings, God made man in His own image, or in His own likeness. This means that God originally gave mankind His Spirit and the means by which to have complete and perfect communication and relationship with God. With this came the gift of living forever, and never facing death. But, Adam, the original man, disobeyed God and suffered the penalty

God had already put in place: Death. Adam first died Spiritually, and then eventually died physically.

The mystery we deal with here is the fact that God, in His infinite mercy and grace, has put in place the perfect processes by which any person can be "reconciled" to God and brought back into God's likeness and image. To be reconciled means to be brought back into a relationship that was originally in place, but was broken.

God's Word given to us in 1 Timothy 3:16 gives us a summary of the processes God put in place in order to give mankind the opportunity to be returned to the perfect relationship that was in place originally with Adam: "And without controversy great is the mystery of godliness: God was manifest in the flesh, justified in the Spirit, seen of angels, preached unto the nations, believed on in the world, received up into glory." This describes the processes God followed and placed in this world in order to bring reconciliation and renewed relationship with sinful humans.

Jesus Christ came in the flesh, in the form of a man, but was truly the incarnation of God. Jesus lived a perfectly sinless life, thus being completely and perfectly justified by the Holiness of God. Jesus Christ was made to be human and was seen and attended to by the angels of God in His humanity. Christ and His glorious Gospel of salvation was introduced to the world and will be preached and presented to all nations of the world.

Every person living on this earth will hear of the opportunity for eternal salvation through faith in Jesus Christ. Those people in this world who truly repent of sin and believe in Christ with complete faith will receive a new birth of the Spirit, and eternal life in Heaven in the future. Jesus Christ defeated death by rising from the grave following His sacrificial death on the Cross. He showed Himself to people believing in Him for 40 days, and then rose up into Heaven, where He returned to be a part of God the Father, leaving His Holy Spirit to be here on earth for those who will trust in Him.

These are the processes that God has put into place for any person who will simply follow God's invitation to come back in Spiritual relationship with Him for all eternity.

While there are other "mysteries" contained in God's Word, we will consider these as the mysteries that reveal the true Kingdom of God to us. In order to understand the Kingdom, we must develop an understanding of these mysteries, which were revealed to us through Jesus Christ and His gift of salvation to eternal life and new life in the Spirit for those of us who claim His gift.

SEVEN

The Kingdom is At Hand

"Repent; for the Kingdom of Heaven is at hand." (Matthew 3:2 and 4:17)

The words of Jesus Christ in Matthew 4:17 are actually the very same words that John the Baptist spoke when he was preaching to all who would listen about the coming of the Messiah, Christ Himself. "In those days came John the Baptist, preaching in the wilderness of Judea, and saying, 'Repent; for the Kingdom of Heaven is at hand'" (Matthew 3:1-2). John was the one who came before the Lord Jesus Christ, helping to prepare the way for Christ to be known to all of the people in those days. The prophet Isaiah foretold of John and his ministry of "preparing the way of the Lord." John the Baptist dedicated his life to preaching the Gospel of Jesus Christ. He preached a message of repentance from sin and faith and trust in the One True Savior: Jesus Christ the Lord. Scripture tells us that John the Baptist dressed in clothing of camel's hair, with a leather belt around his waist, eating food of locusts and wild honey. He truly lived and traveled in the wilderness of those days, going from place to place preaching the Gospel of Salvation to all who would listen.

In fact, people from all around Jerusalem and the country of Judea, including the region around the Jordan River, heard about John and came to hear him. Those who truly believed his message repented of their sins and placed their faith in the Messiah that John preached about. Then, these people followed in believers' Baptism by water as a public example of what the Lord had done in their lives. John even warned those false religious people and any others who refused to believe in Christ that they would face eternal suffering and torment in Hell and the Lake of Fire if they ignored or rejected Jesus Christ and the Salvation He offers.

So, John the Baptist was preaching about the Kingdom of Heaven prior to Jesus Christ actually presenting the Kingdom of Heaven to the world. John was introducing the Kingdom, while Jesus was actually bringing it into reality for the world.

The term "Kingdom of Heaven" used here in Matthew's Gospel account can be literally interpreted as meaning the "Kingdom of the heavens." This term or expression used by John refers to God's absolute rule and authority over the earth and the universe. In this respect, the Kingdom of Heaven can refer to the earth itself, along with the earth's atmosphere, as well as the sun, moon, stars, and galaxies of the universe.

If we use a bit of a contrast with the term "Kingdom of God," we consider the Kingdom of Heaven, as used here with John the Baptist, to be God's Kingdom rule over the people of the earth. Those people who will repent of their sins and trust in Jesus Christ will become a part of the True Kingdom of God, while those who will ignore or reject Christ the Lord and not truly repent of their sins will realize the torment and suffering of Hell. God is the ultimate power and authority for His Kingdom, and only those people who are cleansed and made righteous by repentance of sin and faith in Jesus Christ, will ever realize the perfect joy and peace of being a member of the Kingdom of God, and existing forever in the Kingdom of Heaven to be brought into existence following the destruction of this earth and all the existing "heavens" in the future.

According to C.I. Scofield in his extensive and insightful Study Bible, the Kingdom of Heaven can be presented in three major aspects in the Gospel of Matthew:

1. <u>The Kingdom of Heaven is At Hand:</u> The Kingdom of Heaven is offered to the world in the person of Jesus Christ, as the

King of the Kingdom. The Bible expression "at hand" is not an immediate expression. In other words, the person or thing being referred to as being "at hand" will not necessarily appear immediately, but will be imminent, or certain, in their appearance. When Jesus Christ appeared to the Jewish people, the next thing the people expected to see was the "Davidic Kingdom" as was prophesied in the Old Testament. The Davidic Kingdom was to be a real kingdom here on the earth, actually ruled over by Christ in power and authority. However, the True Kingdom of Heaven was not God's presentation of an earthly kingdom of power, but rather a Spiritual kingdom brought to the people by Christ, His perfect life, His sacrificial death on the Cross, and His resurrection from His death, to be brought back again to His place of power and authority "at the right hand of God the Father" in Heaven.

As a part of fulfilling His Kingdom, God would first allow the rejection and crucifixion of the True King (See Psalms 22 and Isaiah 53). Then God would reveal the long period of the "mystery of the Kingdom" when people of the world would be given the opportunity to repent of sin and trust in Christ the King for cleansing and forgiveness, Spiritual birth, and eternal salvation to an eternal Heaven. God would also provide the earthly time of world-wide preaching of the message of Salvation, being the Gospel (good news) of Jesus Christ as Savior. God would provide for the undisclosed period of time for the fulfillment of His Church, the Body of Christ, taken from the earth into eternity with Him as His redeemed Family.
(See Matthew 13:11 and 17; Ephesians 3:3-12)

2. The Kingdom of Heaven Fulfilled in This Present Age: During this present age on earth, the Kingdom of Heaven is presented in "mysteries", revealing the rule of God in Heaven over the earth and all people between the First Advent of the Lord Jesus Christ and His Second Advent. In other words, between

the time Christ was born here on earth, and the time Christ will come again directly to the earth to take complete control and authority over His eternal Kingdom. Christ will come the Second time and will conquer all evil, destroying Satan's evil, along with the demons, the Antichrist, the False Prophet, and all the people who ever ignored or rejected Christ and His offer of Salvation. Satan will be bound and cast away for 1,000 years, to be loosed for a very brief time and then cast into the Lake of Fire for eternal death and torment (Revelation Chapter 20). In the meantime, the Kingdom of Heaven is here in this earth. The Kingdom is right here among God's people; those who are a part of the True Church and the Family of God. Jesus Christ is the King of the Kingdom of Heaven and gives us His Holy Spirit during this time to guide us, strengthen us, and comfort us.

3. The "mysteries" of the Kingdom of Heaven during this present age are presented to us by the Lord Jesus Christ in part of His teaching while here on earth. Christ presented these "mysteries" in the form of parables. These will be presented in more detail individually in following chapters of this writing.

4. <u>The Kingdom of Heaven as Fulfilled after the Second Coming of Christ:</u> The Kingdom of Heaven will be fulfilled and realized in the future 1,000-year reign of Christ here on earth, known as Christ's Millennial Reign. This will be the future "Millennial Kingdom" aspect of the Kingdom of Heaven as prophesied by Daniel and covenanted by God with David. (Refer to Daniel 2:34-36 and 44-45; 2 Samuel 7:12-16; and Zechariah 12:8). This millennial form of the Kingdom of Heaven will be in the future and will be set up and fulfilled after the return of Jesus Christ to this earth in "power and great glory" (Matthew 24:29 through 25:46; Acts 15:14-17; Matthew 6:33

EIGHT

Mysteries of the Kingdom of Heaven

Jesus Christ spoke many things to the people in the form of parables, which are stories and examples taken from real life and used to illustrate Spiritual principles and truths.

"And He taught them many things by parables." (Mark 4:2)

As mentioned earlier in this writing, a parable is a word-picture using images or stories from daily life to illustrate eternal and Spiritual truths and lessons. The parable actually defines the unknown by using the known. It uses a reality of life to help the listener discover the deeper meaning and underlying truth of a Spiritual principle.

As Jerome, the early biblical scholar and church pioneer observed: "The marrow of a parable is different from the promise of its surface, and like as gold is sought for in the earth, the kernel in a nut, and the hidden fruit in the prickly covering of chestnuts, so in parables we must search more deeply after the divine meaning."

What Jesus did with His use of parables was teach those who would listen and believe in Him what great truths lay in store for all eternity future. He taught them, and each of us in the process, just what God means by bringing His Kingdom to us and presenting us the opportunity to be an integral part of His Kingdom for all eternity.

The parables of Christ have a double meaning. First, there is the literal meaning that is apparent to anyone who has experience or knowledge of the story or example. Then, there is the deeper underlying meaning which illustrates a lesson about God's Truth and God's Kingdom. For example, the parable of the leaven found in Matthew 13:33, relates the example of making flour and dough into bread by including the yeast. This simple illustration actually refers to a person being transformed by God's Truth when he allows God's Word and Spirit to become an integral part of his mind and soul, as the yeast becomes an integral part of the dough in order to be transformed into bread. In addition, when we are "leavened" by God's Spirit, we are called upon to be the leaven that transforms others in our society to accept God's Truth.

Another example is that of the shepherd who loses one sheep out of his flock of one hundred, and goes off to find the one, leaving the ninety-nine unattended. Anyone hearing this parable, and being familiar with tending sheep would wonder why any shepherd would consider leaving ninety-nine to go find one lost sheep. The deeper meaning describes God's sincere concern for His own children who may go astray. With Jesus Christ being considered the Great Shepherd, every single individual is critically important and loved to the extent that He is willing to leave some temporarily in order to rescue the one individual who needs Him.

And so it becomes extremely important for us to be able to consider each of the parables given by the Lord Jesus Christ, and to learn His intended lesson from each. Each parable delivers an especially critical truth and lesson that has eternal implications for each of us. As I mentioned earlier, not everyone will understand Christ's parables. Not everyone will even be interested enough in Christ's teachings to listen, much less understand. But, if you are a person who is interested in having eternal life in Heaven, then you will be one who wants to listen and understand Christ's parables

When Christ said that not everyone would understand the

parables, He was speaking from profound knowledge and experience. Christ knew fully well that not every person would listen to Him or heed His call to repentance, forgiveness, and Salvation. Many people would have closed minds and refuse to consider His Truth. It would not be that they could not intellectually understand His teachings in parables, but rather that they would not care to listen. They would either ignore or even reject Christ's teachings and had already made up their minds that they were not going to listen or believe. The same is true today. Not everyone will be willing to listen to Christ's teachings. Each of His parables is readily available to us for study and growth in God's written Word, the Holy Bible. Many writings, such as the one I present now, are available for reinforcement and support when studying God's Word. There is absolutely no excuse for not understanding the parables of Jesus Christ, just as there is absolutely no excuse for not having Salvation and eternal life through Him.

God will only reveal the secrets and mysteries of His Kingdom to those that are humble and trusting; to those who admit the need of God and His Truth and power in life. The parables of Christ will enlighten each of us if we listen and study them with an open mind and heart.

When reading and studying the parables, it is very important not to become too involved with the details of the story or example. The main point of Spiritual Truth is what really counts. Often the details of the story itself become very clear immediately, while occasionally the story can be a little perplexing. For example, why would a shepherd leave his entire flock unattended to go and find one lost sheep? This detail does not really matter. What really matters is the fact that the "shepherd", being the illustration of Christ Himself, is willing to go and find you as an individual in order to bring you into His "flock" and under His safe care. Any storyteller does not have to make every detail fit perfectly. Don't be overly concerned about small details. Instead, look for the real underlying meaning. In fact, Jesus meant for His parables to provoke a response and some deep thinking on the part of His listeners. If we listen with faith and with humility, we will discover that Jesus has a meaning that speaks to each one of us individually. He wants us to understand the "Mysteries of the Kingdom."

NINE

"Like a Little Child"

"Suffer the little children to come unto Me, and forbid them not: for of such is the Kingdom of God." (Mark 10:14)

One of the earliest descriptions or explanations of the mystery of the Kingdom of God came from Jesus Christ as He told his disciples to always allow little children to come to Him, because it is the innocence and unconditional faith shown by little children that is required for anyone to be a part of the Kingdom of God. Jesus goes on to say: "Whosoever will not receive the Kingdom of God as a little child, he shall not enter therein" (Mark 10:15).

In the Gospel accounts of Matthew, Mark, and Luke we see the time that Jesus was teaching about the way to salvation and to eternal life in the Kingdom of God. The people hearing about Jesus began to bring their young children to Him for His blessings. At one point, Christ's disciples around Him actually rebuked the parents and adults who brought the children to Jesus, thinking that it was just a bother to the Lord. (Refer to Matthew 19:13-15, Mark 10:13-16, and Luke 18:15-17).

When Jesus saw what the disciples were doing, he was displeased and told them to allow the little children to come to Him, reminding them that their innocent faith and trust was the very essence of the Kingdom of God. The New International Version of the Bible says:

"Let the little children come to me, and do not hinder them, for the Kingdom of Heaven belongs to such as these" (Matthew 19:14).

As an interesting note, the Gospel accounts use the terms "Kingdom of Heaven" and "Kingdom of God" almost interchangeably, showing that God considers His *Kingdom* to be inclusive of the Kingdom brought down to earth by Jesus Christ and presented to all mankind as being available for cleansing of sin and for eternal life in Heaven.

What Jesus Christ teaches us here is the fact that any person needs only to repent of sins and trust unconditionally in Jesus as the way by which he or she can receive His cleansing and His blessings for this life and for all eternity in the Heaven to come. He is also confirming that little children, until they have reached the age of accountability, are innocent in the sight of God. Anyone who has observed the innocence and unconditional love of babies and small children will know what I mean. Children are naturally trusting and innocent until they are corrupted and tarnished by the sin of the world, brought upon them by the older people of the world. Jesus helps us to understand that little children, though not competent to fully understand God's blessings, are fully competent to receive God's blessings. In the Kingdom presented by Christ, children and those people willing to show the faith and trust shown by children, are shown God's blessing and mercy.

Interestingly, the practice of infant baptism has been derived from this account in Scripture. In fact, the act of Baptism is purely exemplary and not in any way a physical act that can bestow spiritual qualities on any person. So, it is important to understand that, while innocent children are surely in God's perfect and sovereign will, the act of Baptism should be reserved for the person who understands its true meaning of example and testimony for what the person has decided and acted upon for self. Christ had the perfect opportunity to introduce infant baptism here, but did not.

Christ shows us here that the innocence and trust just like that of a small child is the standard by which any person must come to be a part of the Kingdom ("For of such is the Kingdom of Heaven").

Any person who desires to enter Christ's Kingdom must be trusting, obedient, simple, and pure as a little child (Matthew 18:3). That is why Jesus says, "of such" and not "of these", indicating that it is not the age of the person that really matters, but rather the disposition and character of the person. Any person who would be a true part of the Kingdom of God will show a disregard for selfish motivations, a willingness to turn away from sin and the evil of this world, and a dedication to following Jesus Christ by faith.

When Jesus allowed the little children to come to Him for His blessings, taking them in His arms and placing His hands on them, He showed us His pure humility. He was not above taking special notice of any person, regardless of how small or how weak. He was showing by example just how we ought to be as we follow Him in our life in His Kingdom.

These innocent children were symbolic of the way every person must be in order to be a part of the Kingdom of Heaven. This is what the truly "born again" person must be: just like harmless and innocent children, trusting in Christ alone for strength and guidance in life; free from bitterness and anger; free from pride and self-conceit; free from the hunger for power and worldly ambition; filled with modesty, humility, and love.

It is also clarified by Christ that He does not regard a person's place in life, or source of birth in order to give His blessings. A person may be born of unbelieving parents: it does not matter to God. A person may have committed many grievous sins and even crimes in life: it does not matter to God. What matters to God is whether or not the person is willing to repent of sins and trust by childlike faith in Jesus Christ as Lord.

I have often been asked the question: "Do babies go to Heaven if they die?" I answer in the very strong affirmative. Yes: infants and innocent young children are taken by the Lord to be with Him when they die prematurely. We cannot presume to know God's perfect Will or plan for every human life. But, when Jesus spoke so strongly in support and love for young and innocent children, I know beyond a doubt that the Lord extends His love and His blessings to all of the innocent people of His creation. Those pure and innocent people who have suffered severe brain damage and are not capable of the mental capacity to reach true accountability are also included "as little children." God takes each and every one into His perfect care, just as He does every person who comes to Him "as a little child." At one point, Jesus "called a little child and had him stand among them. And He said: 'I tell you the truth, unless you change and become like little children, you will never enter the Kingdom of Heaven'" (Matthew 18:3).

TEN

The Parable of the Sower

"Behold, a sower went forth to sow...." (Matthew 13:3)

As I pointed out earlier, the "Mysteries of the Kingdom" are presented to us by the Lord Jesus Christ and involve the time period between the Lord's First Advent and His Second Advent. In other words, the time period for the Lord to reveal His mysteries of the Kingdom of Heaven began when Christ was born here on this earth and will end when Christ comes again to this earth to take His rightful place as King of the Kingdom of Heaven. Meanwhile, Christ has actually brought His Kingdom of Heaven down to this earth to make available to all people who will listen, understand, and believe His Word. This time is taking place now and will continue until Christ comes again.

Christ reveals these mysteries to us in eight different stories, or parables found in the Gospel of Matthew, Chapter Three.

As we begin studying these teachings that clarifies the Kingdom for us, we will consider parts presented by the Lord Jesus Christ. The first part includes the first four parables. These were presented by Christ to the multitudes, or a great number of people gathered in a place. Jesus was going to where the people could hear Him. He was on a mountainside or somewhere that He was surrounded by a large crowd of people. Jesus spoke four different parables to these crowds regarding the mysteries of the Kingdom of Heaven. These first four parables deal with the Kingdom as viewed from a human standpoint.

Christ is saying that this is the way that the Kingdom looks down here in this world. This is the way that the Kingdom looks to us from its external and visible form. This is the way the Kingdom will work in your life here on earth if you choose to become a part of the Kingdom by accepting and believing His Words, and making Christ the central focal point of your life.

The next four parables describe the Kingdom of Heaven from God's point of view. These stories describe what God is going to do. They reveal God's internal secrets.

The first parable that Christ gives us is the Parable of the Sower. A "sower" is a person who plants, or sows, seed. In this story, Christ gives us a very common setting involving a person who goes out to plant seed. When the person went out and planted, "some of the seeds fell by the wayside," meaning that these seeds simply were scattered on the ground in the process of throwing the seed in areas the sower intended. These seeds simply lay on the surface of the ground and the birds came along and ate them, not giving them a chance to take root and grow.

Some of the seed being sown fell on "stony places" where they did not have much earth for nourishment and root. These seeds actually developed short roots and came up but, because they did not have sufficient soil, their root system could not survive. The sun came out and dried them up and they "withered away."

Some of the seed "fell among thorns" and when the thorns grew thick, choked out the good plants before they had a chance to mature and bear fruit.

But the rest of the seed went into "good ground", grew, and even "brought forth fruit." Some of the plants that grew brought forth a great amount of fruit (a hundredfold), while the rest of the good plants brought forth various amounts of fruit.

But, the point here is that the fruit that was planted in "good ground" actually produced fruit. Christ told this story and then announced: "Anyone who truly wants to hear and understand this Spiritual Truth, let him listen, understand, and believe."

In this story, three out of the four circumstances presented met with defeat and failure. This is very significant here in this world. Much of what we see in this world is negative and goes against God and His Will for people. As we know from God's Word; "God is not willing that anyone should perish, but that all should come to repentance" (2 Peter 3:9).

When we consider the Kingdom of Heaven here on earth, it deals with antagonism, bitterness, and even hatred. Sometimes it even seems that the whole world has turned against Almighty God who made it. If you are not very careful you will fall into the same kind of despair and antagonism. You must guard against the hatred and antagonism of the world by listening to God's Truth. Listen carefully to these parables and their inner teachings so that you can be the "good ground" on which the seed of the Gospel falls and takes root.

So, we see in this first parable taught by the Lord, that even the chosen Apostles following Christ did not fully understand what He was teaching. They asked Jesus, "Why do You speak to them in parables?" Jesus answered them and explained how critical it is that the people who would hear and believe His words were the ones who needed to understand clearly. Others, who would not listen or believe the Lord and His teachings, would not understand these parables and would not be able to act against them or repudiate them.

With this early use of parables, Jesus thought it was very important to clarify the underlying meaning of the story more directly. In Matthew 3:18 Christ begins to clarify for them. He explains; "When anyone hears the Word of the Kingdom, and does not understand it, then the *wicked one* comes and takes away the words that were spoken. This means that Satan actually acts to mislead and misguide a person who is first hearing the message of Salvation and grace offered by God through Jesus Christ. The *seed* is actually representing the Word of God to people. God's Word tells us that if we are willing to repent of our sins and trust by faith in Jesus Christ as Lord and Savior, we will be born again of the Spirit, become God's own child, and will inherit eternal life in Heaven with Him. This Gospel message is the seed. The person hearing the message is the *ground* in which the seed is sown, or planted. The person who hears this Sacred Message will react like one of the types of soil in which the seed is sown. The person who allows the message to be muted and distorted by Satan is the one who received the message, or seed, "by the wayside."

The person that receives the seed "in stony places" is the person that hears the message of Salvation and "immediately receives it with joy" but has no root within himself. In other words, the person is initially receptive, but when the world and sin presents some trials and troubles and persecution because of the "Christian way of life," he falls back into the world and its life. The initial message of Salvation was not taken seriously by this person and there was never any true repentance and faith in Christ. Many people in our world today fall into this category. Most people have heard the Gospel message of Salvation.

Many have even responded initially, thinking that they have done all they need to do. But then these people fall back into their worldly life and ignore Christ and what He has done for them on the Cross.

The person that receives the "seed among the thorns" is the person that hears the message of Salvation but allows the "care of this world, and the deceitfulness of riches, to choke the Word, and he becomes unfruitful" (Matthew 3:22). This type of person is also very common in our world today. This is the person that heard the Gospel message, probably at an early age, and responded as he or she felt they should. Some responded because they were expected to. Some responded because they were temporarily enthused and motivated by the attention they received. Some responded without truly understanding why they were doing it. But, as time passed, these people cared more about the world and their own life, work, and pleasure. They may care more about wealth and success than they do about Jesus Christ. They may care more about their selfish use of personal time spent on hobbies and pleasures than they do about serving Jesus Christ here in the world. These are people who may even consider themselves to be "saved" and feel that they are okay for eternity. These will be the very people that the Lord speaks about when He says: "Not everyone who says to Me, Lord, Lord, will enter into the Kingdom of Heaven, but only the person who does the will of

My Father, Who is in Heaven. Many will say to me in that day, Lord, Lord, have we not prophesied in your name? And in your name have cast out demons? And in your name done many wonderful works? And then I will profess to them, I never knew you; depart from Me, you who work iniquity" (Matthew 7:21-23).

But, after these three failures, there is great news! The person who "receives the seed in good ground" is the person who hears the Word of God for Salvation, understands it, and takes it into his or her inner being, trusting totally by faith in Jesus Christ as Lord, and will be one of those children of God who "bears fruit" in life. The "fruit" is the outward evidence that the person is born of the Spirit. The life born of the Spirit will reflect the "fruit of the Spirit." The person bearing fruit will share the message of Salvation with other people in the world. This will be the person who can't help but proclaim the good news that Jesus Christ has cleansed them from their sins and has given them the precious gift of eternal Salvation. This will be the person who is genuine and earnest in serving Christ here in this world. This will be the person who reflects the "fruit of the Spirit" spoken of by the Apostle Paul in Galatians: "But the fruit of the Spirit is love, joy, peace, patience, gentleness, goodness, faith, meekness, temperance: against such there is no law" (Galatians 5:22). These people are the true children of God. They are the true members of the Body of Christ. They are the true Church. These people will bear the fruit of the Holy Spirit in their lives in various degrees. Some will bear more than others. Some will be asked by God to serve in more ways than others. But all will be chosen to serve in some way that will glorify the Lord Jesus Christ in their life.

The Lord makes a point of teaching us that there will be opposition in the inner souls of the people that hear this message of Salvation. Your life will be, or already has been one of these types of soil.

You should realize that there is only one good type in the examples given. You must be the "good ground" in your reception of the Gospel of Salvation in order to be born of the Spirit and belong to God for all eternity.

Don't make the mistake of being mistaken. You can be wrong in your life and not truly have taken the time to even realize it. Take the opportunity now to examine your life and your very soul. You should have no doubts whatsoever regarding your eternal state of existence if you are truly born of the Spirit. But the only way you can truly know is in the Spirit.

Many people may "think" that they are saved and will be in Heaven when they die. You think with your mind or your brain and your mind can be fooled. It should be obvious to anyone who cares that you can be mistaken. You can be fooled in your thinking. I do not believe there is any person living in this world that has not been fooled in their thinking at some point in their life. Everyone has been fooled. Everyone has had the wrong thinking at some point.

Many people may "feel" like they are saved and will be in Heaven when they die. You feel with your emotions and your emotions are simply a result of your thinking process. For example, there can be an incident that happens in your life that makes you feel a certain type of emotion, while other people may have the opposite or different emotional reaction to the same event. Many people become emotional when hearing certain types of speeches, seeing certain movies, or hearing certain stories. What was your emotion when you heard the Gospel of Salvation first presented to you? Did you become emotional and react emotionally, only to move on in your life without having truly been born again of the Spirit? There is nothing wrong with emotions. They are a very natural part of human nature. But emotions can lead you to actions that do not have significant and long-lasting results.

You may be one who says "I believe that I am saved." I should not have to explain this condition in too much detail. How often have you believed something that is just not true? I was recently asked the question: "Is there really such a place as Heaven and Hell?" Of course I answered: "Absolutely!" Another person joining in the conversation said: "Well, you believe there is a Heaven and a Hell, but you don't really know for sure." I explained my certainty of truly knowing by explaining that "believing" is a part of your thinking and emotions, and they can be fooled because they are part of your flesh and humanity. Any person can only truly "know" in the Spirit. If you stop at just believing, then you are stopping short of knowing in your Spirit. Many people in this world really believe they are OK when they are not. In order to absolutely know the things of the Spirit, you must be born again of the Spirit. In order to truly know the things of God, such as His mysteries of the *Kingdom*, you must be in the Spirit.

Some people actually "know" that they are saved and will be in Heaven when they die. How do you really know? You know in your Spirit. Your Spirit can't be fooled. Your Spirit is born within you only when you truly repent of your sins and truly trust in Jesus Christ as your Lord and King. Therefore, your Spirit bears witness with the Holy Spirit of God that you are His child. There is no fooling God. You can fool yourself and others, but never God. As we examine other parables and Spiritual Truth from the Lord Jesus Christ, place yourself in each part of the story to see where you fit. It is eternally critical that you are in the right place: IN CHRIST JESUS!

ELEVEN

The Parable of the Tares

The parables of Jesus Christ serve to explain to us just what the Kingdom of Heaven is like. Christ said: "Many prophets and righteous men have desired to see those things which you see, and they have not seen them; and to hear those things which you hear, and have not heard them." So, Christ says, listen and learn.

The second parable that Christ shares is the parable of the tares. *Tare* is the ancient term for *weed*. Tares are weeds that are not good for anything except ruining the growth and production of valuable and worthwhile crops. In Christ's time wheat was one of the staple crops, being most valuable to the people for food. If a crop of wheat had too many weeds growing in it, the weeds would choke out the wheat and the crop would not be productive for the needed food. The growth of tares, or weeds, in a promising crop of wheat is very threatening and potentially damaging. In fact, the growth of too many weeds in any crop will eventually destroy the good crop.

In this parable, the Lord is illustrating the effects of the evil of Satan in the lives of people who have had the Gospel of Salvation shared and "implanted" in their lives. Some people will continue to grow and produce the Gospel of Jesus Christ in their lives, while others will allow Satan and the sin of this world to "choke them out," destroying the "good seed" of the Gospel of Jesus Christ and the Salvation He offers.

Christ begins this parable by pointing out that this story is "likened" to the Kingdom of Heaven. This significant teaching is sharing just what the Kingdom of Heaven is like. The Kingdom of Heaven in this world is shared with all people. Some people will take it and apply it to their very inner soul, becoming born again of the Spirit and securing their place in Heaven for all eternity. Many people will consider the message, but will allow Satan and the world to take control of their lives, thus quenching the effects of the Holy Spirit in their lives. The people that allow the "tares" of Satan to impact their lives will be those who are condemned to Hell and the Lake of Fire in the end.

Not only is it difficult to see the good seed of the Gospel of Salvation produced and growing in the lives and souls of people, it is difficult to even get the message of Salvation across to so many people. Many will not even listen and consider the Word of God leading to Salvation. Satan will harden their hearts and create a depravity and sinfulness that is innately in the soul and life of many human beings.

This parable tells us that, when God's "seed" is sown in the world, the field (the world) is also oversown with tares by Satan and his evil influence. We find that to be true everywhere in the world, not just in America. Anywhere you see people working for God and sharing the good news of Salvation, you will also see the strong influence of Satan, trying to nullify God's Word in the minds of people: tares among the wheat. You can see the weeds growing up in the lives of individuals. You can see the weeds of Satan's influence growing up in the lives of families. You can see the weeds growing up in every city and town and village on this earth. It is the "oversowing" of Satan.

In this parable, compared to the parable of the sower, the "good seed" is not the Word, but rather that which the Word has produced. The "good seed" are the children of the Kingdom who have been born again of the Spirit.

The "tares" are the people living for Satan and his influence. These people may appear to be good people. They may even be people who are active in local churches. They will be people who befriend true children of God and bring sinful influence upon them. They are often people who don't even realize that they are not "good seed." They are often people who think they are okay and go on living their lives in ignorance of true Salvation.

The Apostle Peter presented this great Spiritual Truth in another way: "Forasmuch as you know that you were not redeemed with corruptible things, like silver and gold, from your vain manner of life received by tradition from your fathers, but with the precious blood of Christ, as of a Lamb without blemish and without spot, Who truly was foreordained before the foundation of the world, but was shown to us (manifest) in these last times for you, who by Him do believe in God, Who raised Him up from the dead and gave Him Glory, so that your faith and hope might be in God. Seeing that you have purified your souls in obeying the Truth through the Spirit unto unfeigned love of the brethren, see that you love one another with a pure heart fervently, Being born again, not of corruptible seed, but of incorruptible, by the Word of God, which lives and abides forever" (1 Peter 1:18-23).

So, the Word of God produced "good seed" in the lives of people, and "while men slept" the "enemy came and sowed weeds among the good wheat, and went on his way." When the wheat was coming up in the lives of people producing the good fruit of the Spirit, then the weeds of the sinful world came along also. We see that the "servants", being those people who are striving to serve the Lord, saw the influence of Satan as the weeds, and came to the Lord and the others bringing the message of Salvation and said: "Didn't you put out the "good seed" of the Word of God in the "field" of the world to all the people? Where did the weeds of Satan come from?

The "good seed" of people who truly know God as Heavenly Father and are truly serving the Lord Jesus Christ, know that the evil influence of the world comes from Satan and his sinful influence. Where children of the Kingdom of God are gathered, there among them will be the "children of the wicked one," who profess to be children of the Kingdom but are not genuine. In outward ways, these children of the world and Satan may actually be like the true children of God, but are not genuine in their souls. They have never been born of the Spirit, and are hypocrites. In the end, only the angels of the Lord can be trusted to separate them. So great is Satan's power of deception that the weeds, or tares, often really think of themselves as being true children of the Kingdom (Matthew 7:21-23). In fact, many other stories and illustrations present this condition of mingling in the world (Matthew 22:11-14; Matthew 25:1-13 and 14-30; Luke 18:10-14; and Hebrews 6:4-9). In fact, this is characteristic of Matthew's Gospel writing from Chapter 13 to the end.

Then, Christ shares a most profound Truth with us. The good people serving God then suggest that the Lord go out and gather the sinful part of the world up and destroy them (Matthew 13:28). But, the Lord says "No; in case you should make a mistake while you are destroying the sinful ones, and destroy the good people with them, let both grow together until the time of harvest; and in the time of harvest I will say to the reapers, 'Gather together first the weeds, and bind them in bundles to burn them, but gather the wheat into My barn" (Matthew 13:29-30).

In other words, the Lord says that the good people of God and the sinful people of this world will go on living together until the final Day of Judgment, when the Lord will judge the "wicked dead." The sinful people of this world, including all those who ignored or rejected the Salvation offered by Jesus Christ, will be put together and will be cast into the eternal Lake of Fire, where there will be extreme suffering for all time to come. The children of God will be brought into everlasting peace and comfort in Heaven ("into His barn").

This parable of the wheat and the tares is not actually a description of the world in general, but rather describes that part of the world that professes to be within the Kingdom. It describes those who profess to be part of the Kingdom but are really false in their identity and in their lives, as compared to those who are truly born again of the Spirit and subsequently true children of the Kingdom of Heaven. They are in opposition in the world, just as weeds and wheat are in opposition in a field.

When Jesus Christ returns to this earth to reign as King and Lord, this parable will have its fulfillment. The wicked will be destroyed, as illustrated by the burning of the tares. The Church, which will be translated, or taken up, before the Tribulation here on earth, will be gathered into the millennial Kingdom of Heaven, together with those living believers who have survived the Tribulation period, along with the righteous men and women of all the previous ages, as illustrated by the gathering of the wheat into the barn.

(Refer to Matthew 13:43; 24:13; 25:31-34).

TWELVE

The Parable of the Mustard Seed

"The Kingdom of Heaven is like a grain of mustard seed." (Matthew 13:31-32)

Have you ever seen a mustard seed? I have seen them. In fact, occasionally I see a girl who will be wearing a necklace with a little crystal ball on it. Inside the little ball will be a mustard seed. This necklace is usually made to signify the Lord's saying: "If you have faith the size of a grain of mustard seed nothing shall be impossible for you" (Matthew 17:20). The mustard seed is one of the smallest seeds in nature, but as it is planted and grows, it grows and matures into a very large and significant tree; not just a small bush, but a great tree. The mustard tree can grow to a height of 12 feet.

The Lord is giving us a very real Truth in this parable. The inner meaning of this story signifies the small handful of men on the Sea of Galilee who chose to stop everything they were doing in life and follow Jesus. These men faithfully followed and learned from the Lord. They eventually became the very "seed" Christ chose to use in order to grow His Kingdom here on earth. Christ chose these men to be the very foundation of His Church in this world. It is through the preaching and teaching of these few men that the entire world has heard the Gospel of Salvation. Like the great mustard tree, the branches of Christianity have spread throughout the earth and have covered the civilized world. As we know from the Lord's prophecy, the entire world will eventually hear the Gospel and will have the opportunity to surrender to the Lordship of Jesus Christ. From a very small beginning, the Kingdom of Heaven has been spread across the earth, like a tiny mustard seed grows into a great tree with spreading branches.

When the mustard seed grew into a great tree, the birds came and lived in the branches of it. In a way, this can signify that the "tree of Christianity" provides lodging for the many people of the world who choose to come and be a part of it. The Kingdom of Heaven provides safety and security for every member.

In another viewpoint, the tree provided a place for every bird to come and make their nests and make the tree foul and dirty. This viewpoint brings out the foul and dirty world that always finds the "branches" of Christianity and attempts to make it foul and dirty along with it. The world is vile and sinful and always seeks a way to try to pollute the true Church, the same way many birds in a tree can have a fouling and polluting affect. I know a place where there is a magnificent old spruce tree. It was a huge and beautiful tree when I first saw it. Over the years, buzzards have been roosting in the tree. At times there have been up to thirty or more buzzards in the tree. The mess these birds leave is really horrible. I know this is just a part of God's nature but, nevertheless, the impact of these buzzards on the tree has been very negative, just as the impact of the sinful world is very negative on the life of a Christian, and on the Ch

In one way, the parable is used to explain the Kingdom of Heaven in the world. In another way, the story explains the Kingdom within each individual believer. We should keep in mind that the people Jesus was speaking to were Jewish. The Jews, or Israelites, were God's chosen people. Through the Old Testament years, God promised that He was going to send a Savior to the world. Many of the Jewish people misunderstood what this meant. They thought God was going to send a mighty king to rescue them from the evil of the Roman government, like God rescued their ancestors from the stronghold of slavery with the Egyptians. They expected this Savior to set them physically free by military force. But, of course, this is not what God meant. God was sending the Savior to set people free from their own sin.

In this parable, Jesus was telling all who would listen that their way of life and thinking was not God's way at all. God directed them to be meek and humble, just like Jesus was when He came to earth.

In fact, Jesus Christ Himself started out as a living example of His parable of the mustard seed. As one man, Christ began to preach and teach the secrets of the Kingdom of Heaven which He was personally bringing to the world. As He continued to preach, in combination with His many miracles of healing, His fame began to grow steadily until multitudes of people were coming to hear Him.

Following His death and resurrection, Christ directed His few chosen disciples to spread His Gospel of Salvation and love throughout the world (Matthew 28:19-20). Along with Jesus, these few were like the tiny seed. Within the huge masses in the world, they were just a tiny seed, but they were full of potential, just like the mustard seed. Within them lay the potential for production into a fruitful tree. As the "mustard seed" of their ministry continued, it grew into more and more production of "seed" until it has spread throughout the world. Disciples of the original disciples created even more disciples, even to this day. The Kingdom has grown just like Jesus said it would.

By the same token, the parable of the mustard seed can also describe how God's Kingdom grows in the life of each believer. When a person puts his or her faith and trust in Jesus Christ, the Holy Spirit comes in to the soul and Spirit of the person to live and grow. The birth of the Spirit within a person is like the mustard seed being planted in the ground. No one can see it from the outside, but it is absolutely there. At first the believer may not feel a lot different, but the Holy Spirit is most powerful. He has the power to transform the person, just like the seed has the natural power to become a huge plant. The full-grown mustard tree produces more fruit and more seed. It makes branches suitable for birds to live in and rest on. It makes seeds that are made into good food as well as becoming more seed to produce more trees. So the Holy Spirit produces good things in the life of the true believer. The Spiritual fruit shows in the life of the true child of God. If the person is truly born of the Spirit, the fruit of that person's life will show the Fruit of the Spirit (Galatians 5:22-25), just like the mustard tree will produce mustard seed.

Like the growth of the tiny seed into a large tree, the growth is somewhat slow. You won't see changes overnight or immediately, but in time, the influence and power of the Holy Spirit in the believer's life will grow to great stages. Before the new child of God even realizes it, his or her life can become so much different than their former life of sin.

When you repent of your sin and trust in Jesus Christ as your Lord and Savior, God's Holy Spirit enters you, giving you new life in your Spirit. You become a new person, or a new creation, as God's Word tells us (2 Corinthians 5:17). As a new person in Christ, the new believer will need to grow and mature.

By God's power and will in your life, the Spirit grows and matures in you little by little until you become mature enough to bear the Fruit of the Spirit in your life, while bringing other lives into the Kingdom of Heaven.

THIRTEEN

The Parable of the Leaven

> ***"The Kingdom of Heaven is like leaven, which a woman took, and placed in three measures of meal, until the entire dough was leavened." (Matthew 13:33)***

This brief statement by the Lord Jesus Christ has been interpreted and misinterpreted throughout the 2000+ years since His sacred teachings. I will present two interpretations regarding this sacred parable. What was Christ saying here? What did He really mean by His parable of leaven?

If people take this profound Biblical statement by the Lord at face value on a human level, then we hear the interpretation of a sweet and positive nature. We often hear people who are professing to be Bible teachers, and even pastors and preachers, teaching this parable as one of encouragement and positive growth for the Christian kingdom. One such teacher even introduced his or her interpretation by saying: "I love eating bread or rolls with yeast (leaven) in it. Yeast makes bread taste delicious……It only takes a very small amount of yeast to puff up a large amount of dough……This parable about the yeast (leaven) was very much like the parable of the mustard seed. The main point of both parables was this: Sometimes things that start out small end up really huge! These parables must have been a great encouragement to Jesus' disciples who had joined the kingdom when it was very small on earth." This teacher went on to say: "Sometimes we get discouraged when we are trying to live out the kingdom life......These parables should encourage you very much. While we might not be able to "see" the growth of the kingdom every day, it is growing – both in the world, and in the hearts of the believers. We could not stop the growth of God's kingdom any more than we could take the yeast out of a batch of dough, or force a mustard plant back into its seed!"

Now, this teaching is very nice and not altogether without merit. Certainly, we can consider this interpretation and give it some value in our study. But, this is not what the Lord was really saying. In fact, we must realize that Jesus Christ knew God's Word without question or variance. Jesus Christ *IS* God's Word! He even went on to explain His parable in Matthew 16:6-12, leaving no doubt as to His true meaning.

In order to identify exactly what Christ was saying, we should examine God's Word in total. We must understand that the Lord Jesus Christ would never contradict His own Word. The term may be used in a different context, but it will always be clarified if we listen closely and understand. Whenever He uses a term like *leaven*, in a figurative sense, it will always carry the same meaning as God's Word has given it. Whenever the Lord uses an example of a *woman,* also in a figurative sense, it will always carry the same meaning as God's Word gives it. The true meaning will be in a Spiritual context. The meaning of *leaven*, in a physical context, is good, and leavened bread does taste good. But the leaven Christ refers to is not good at all. Keep in mind the reason we use unleavened bread in our observance of the Lord's Supper (Communion).

After all, "God is not the author of confusion" (1 Corinthians 14:33). From the very beginning of God's Word, the figurative *woman* always represented the harlot, such as that woman in Thyatira: that Jezebel, or that harlot: Babylon. In every case, the *woman* represents the evil influence upon the Kingdom of God. (Refer to Isaiah 1:21; Jeremiah 2:20; Ezekiel 16; Ezekiel 23; Hosea 2; Revelation 17; and Revelation 18).

Leaven, as a symbolic or figurative substance, is always represented in the Old Testament in an evil sense. It is never mentioned positively. In fact, that is the very reason that the Hebrew people were instructed to eat "unleavened" bread during the Holy days. Beginning in Genesis 19:3, we see Lot meeting the two angels sent by God to Sodom. Lot pleaded with them to come into his house and finally convinced them to do so. Lot served them "a feast, and did bake unleavened bread, and they did eat."

The use of the figurative *leaven* in the New Testament has the symbolic meaning of "malice or wickedness" and is in contrast to "sincerity and truth." In 1 Corinthians 5:6-8 we learn of the real meaning of figurative leaven as Paul teaches us: "Your glorying is not good. Don't you know that a little leaven leavens the whole lump? Purge out, therefore, the old leaven, so that you may be a new lump, because you are unleavened. For even Christ, our Passover, is sacrificed for us. Therefore, let us keep the feast, not with old leaven, neither with the leaven of malice or wickedness, but with the unleavened *bread* of sincerity and truth." Here, as in all other places in God's Word, the leaven is symbolic of "malice or wickedness." The figurative bread is symbolic of the figurative wheat or flour used in Scripture to represent the Lord and His Church, made up of born-again believers. Spiritually, if you are a born-again child of God through your repentance of sin and faith in Jesus Christ, then you are a part of the Spiritual Body of Christ and a part of the "bread of life."

In reality, the teaching of Christ in this parable is one of corruption and crisis within the true Church in this world. The use of the term *leaven* by Jesus in this parable represents an evil doctrine coming into the sacred Kingdom of God in this world. The *woman* represents the evil influence of the Pharisees, Sadducees, and Herodians in the world at that time. They were religious in their behavior, but their religion was hypocritical. They did not love the Lord. In fact, they hated Christ and rejected Him totally, finally crucifying Him on the cruel Cross. The *leaven* of the Pharisees was their hypocritical religion which did not honor or please God, but was accepted in the world. The *leaven* of the Sadducees was their rejection of Christ as the true Messiah and Savior to the world. The *leaven* of the Herodians was worldliness and sinfulness in the sight of God. The use of the term *leaven* in the figurative sense is consistent throughout all of Scripture and the Lord Jesus Christ is always consistent in His Word.

In fact, the Lord actually explained His meaning of this parable to the disciples in Matthew 16:6-12, leaving no doubt as to His true meaning. Jesus said to them: "Take heed and beware of the leaven of the Pharisees and of the Sadducees." The disciples actually thought at first that Jesus was admonishing them for forgetting to bring bread along on their journey. But Jesus, knowing and perceiving their thoughts and concerns said: "O you people of little faith, why do you reason among yourselves because you have forgotten to bring bread? Don't you understand yet? Don't you remember how I fed the five thousand people with only five loaves of bread, and had so much left over? Don't you remember how I fed four thousand people with only seven loaves of bread, and had so much left over? How is it that you don't understand that I was not talking to you about actual bread, but I was warning you to beware of the *leaven* or evil influence of the Pharisees and Sadducees? Then they understood that Christ was not telling them to beware of the actual leaven in bread, but of the doctrine of the Pharisees and of the Sadducees." In other words, the Apostles finally understood that Jesus was not being physical and worldly in His teaching. He was being Spiritual, just as His whole nature was Spiritual.

The woman in this parable is a symbol of evil. The meal represents our Lord, just as meal, wheat, and flour represent our blessed Savior and His Gospel here in this earth. The evil woman took the evil doctrine and influence she has and put it into God's work here on earth. This evil influence has spread out over the years, just as Christ said it would. The evil influence of Satan and his worldly doctrine of sin and disobedience to God is the leaven and has corrupted God's Kingdom to a great degree.

Keep in mind that these first four parables found in Christ's teachings in Matthew's Gospel account have to do with the Kingdom of Heaven as we see it down here in this world. The Lord Jesus Christ is giving His followers warnings as to the powerful and evil influence they will encounter in this world. His teachings apply to us in this modern world as well. We have clear warning: the Church can be corrupted. The sacred doctrine of faith in Jesus Christ can be corrupted. The true Body of Christ and the true Kingdom of God can be distorted to so many people by the evil influence (leaven) of Satan and his instruments in this world. Worldliness, compromise, atheism, greed, selfishness, and every vile thing known to the human heart makes up the *leaven* of this world, and it seeps and creeps into every facet of God's Kingdom.

We need only look at history to realize the truth of Christ's prophecy in this parable. Take any recording of history in our history books and you can learn of the growth of Christendom in this world. In the eastern part of the civilized world, it was called the Greek Orthodox Church. That church finally became so evil and so corrupt that its symbol in 1917 became the Greek Orthodox priest Rasputin, who had more power over the Czar (ruler) Nicholas II than all of the armies or citizens of the entire Russian empire. Then, as history records, Corinsky and socialist rebels murdered Rasputin and the entire family of Nicholas II. They closed down the churches and they outlawed the seminaries, their monasteries, and their priests. Of all the corruptions in the Russian empire, the most corrupt became the church itself. The priests were used by the new Czar to spy on the people in order to suppress, oppress, and persecute them. Finally, God determined when it was enough and used the atheistic infidels to destroy them. Now, there is just a small remnant of the old corrupt church, giving us a living example of Christ's parable of the leaven.

In the Western church, we see the Latin, or Roman influence: The Roman Catholic Church. If you truthfully consider history, you will find the internal structure of the Roman Catholic Church to be one of the most murderous, adulterous, vile, and corrupt organizations our world has ever known. At a point, the Catholic Church even sold the church offices or positions. You could become a bishop if you had enough money to buy it. The entire establishment became corrupt in their doctrine, and in their life and practice in this world. As we discover in study of the Revelation, the Roman Catholic Church will actually be so evil as to be the very source of the False Prophet of our future world Tribulation times. The Roman Catholic Church is actually the prophetic evil Babylon of the future. I refer you to the Scriptural Book of Revelation, and as a study supplement, to my book entitled: *The Ultimate End.*

Then we consider the Protestant Reformation in our world's history, and what has happened to our Protestant churches throughout the world. An account by W.A. Criswell, the great Bible preacher and teacher of over 60 years in Texas, as the Pastor of First Baptist Church of Dallas, gives us clear insight. He shared that one of the deacons in his church sent him an article out of a current newspaper. In it was listed all of the things that the modern denominations believe. There was a significant percentage of the Protestant denominations of America that disavow and disbelieve practically every one of the doctrines of faith that established the true Church given to us by the Lord Jesus Christ and His chosen Apostles and their teachings. Shockingly, there are even seminary professors who don't even believe in God! We commonly see articles and publications espousing a "God is Dead" philosophy. There is rampant corruption and distortion in the Protestant ministry and in our theological schools.

Dr. Criswell went on to share the story of John D. Rockefeller, Sr. giving $600,000 to match an offering of $400,000 from Baptist people throughout America in order to start the Morgan Park Baptist Theological Seminary within the organization of Chicago University, for the purpose of evangelizing the heartland of America. History relates that, the very beginning of the school and Rockefeller's millions of dollars of support saw the beginning of corruption and evil influence, literally destroying the school and its entire purpose. The Chicago University became, and remains, a symbol of atheism and infidelity and denial of faith in God and the Lord Jesus Christ.

This grave but realistic example of Christ's teachings in His parable of the leaven gave rise to an editorial in one of the newspapers of Chicago: "We are struck with the hypocrisy and treachery of these attacks on Christianity. This is a free country and a free age, and men can say what they choose about religion. But this is not what we arraigned these divinity professors for. Is there no place in which to assail Christianity but in a divinity school? Is there no one to write infidel books except professors of Christian theology? Is a theological seminary an appropriate place for a general massacre of Christian doctrine? We are not championing either Christianity or infidelity, but only condemning infidels masquerading as men of God and Christian teachers."

A man named Bob Ingersoll used to travel all over America making infidel talks. He would declare the mistakes of God, attacking the Bible and the divinity of Jesus Christ. After he stopped touring and speaking almost totally Mr. Ingersoll was asked: "Why don't you do it anymore?" Bob Ingersoll replied: "Because I don't need to. I don't need to do that anymore. These professors in the seminary and in the divinity schools are making a better shambles of religion than I could ever do it."

This is just what the Lord Jesus Christ was talking about in His parable of the leaven. As the true faith in God grows and as the Kingdom of Heaven is extended, there will be leaven of evil influence corrupting the doctrine and teachings of the Lord Jesus Christ.

FOURTEEN

The Parable of the Hidden Treasure

"The Kingdom of Heaven is like treasure hidden in a field, which when a man has found it, he hides it, and being so glad to have found it he goes and sells all that he has, and buys the whole field." (Matthew 13:44)

As mentioned earlier, the last four parables of Jesus Christ are parables concerning the Kingdom of Heaven as relating to the secrets and mysteries of God. The first four relate to the Kingdom of Heaven as it is here on this earth. These last four relate to the Kingdom of Heaven in a truly Spiritual sense.

There have been two major interpretations of this parable over the years. Perhaps the most popular of the interpretations presents the buyer of the field as being a sinful person who is seeking Jesus Christ. As we clearly see in another parable found in Matthew 13:38, (the parable of the sower - Chapter Nine), the field in Christ's parables represents the world. In this interpretation the sinner does not buy the field, or the world, but forsakes the world in order to gain Christ. In fact, the sinner has nothing to sell in order to buy the field. Another contradiction in this interpretation is present when we consider that Jesus Christ is not for sale; neither is He hidden in the field of the world. Additionally, no sinner, having found Jesus Christ in the first place, would ever consider hiding Him again. In fact, as we see in Mark 7:24 and Acts 4:20, it is not possible for the Lord Jesus Christ to be hidden in this world. At every point of this profound parable, this interpretation breaks down.

The true interpretation gives us a beautiful representation of the Lord Jesus Christ paying the ultimate price of His own life on the Cross as the Supreme sacrifice for the purchase of the world and all sinners. In other words, the field is the world which was purchased by the Lord at the ultimate cost of His own blood and life in order that He might have the treasure. The *treasure hidden in a field* represents God's original treasure of Israel in this world from the Old Testament times, while also representing each and every person of the world who repents of sin and trusts totally in Jesus Christ as Lord and Savior, thus becoming a Spiritual Jew and joint heir with Jesus Christ, being born again of the Spirit. So, the treasure represents the true Church, or Body of Christ, made up of all who believe in Christ and have been born of the Spirit. The Old Testament Israel is presented in Exodus 19:5 and Psalms 135:4, and the New Testament "remnant" of Israel is presented in Romans 11:5, being made up of those who have become a part of the remnant of Israel "according to the election of grace." Those people who make up the true remnant are no longer counted strictly as Jews but as members of "one body" together with the saved Gentiles from all nations. (Refer to Galatians 3:28; Ephesians 2:14-18; Ephesians 4:4; Ephesians 1:18; and Hebrews 12:2). As part of the Body of Christ, having been born again of the Spirit, this treasure becomes "Christ's inheritance" and "Christ's joy."

And so, the true interpretation shows us the treasure hidden in a field as being the Nation of Israel and all people from the world who trust fully in Jesus Christ, becoming His True Church. This treasure is hidden in the field which represents the world itself.

The "man" finding the treasure, hiding the treasure, and giving all that He has in order to purchase the entire field of the world is the Lord Jesus Christ. Jesus came to this earth in the form of man in order to find the treasure, hide it in the world, and give His life as the ultimate sacrifice to purchase the treasure from within the world.

The beautiful Spiritual truth of this parable shows us that the Lord Jesus Christ has already "purchased the field" by giving His life for the entire world. John 3:16 tells us that "God loved the world so much that He gave His only begotten Son so that whoever believes in Him will not have to perish and suffer, but will have everlasting life." Christ died for the entire world, including those people who will reject and ignore Him and His sacrifice for them. Even those people who deny the very existence of God have been given the opportunity to become a part of the "treasure" which is the Body of Christ, the True Church. Christ has already paid the price and those of us who have repented of sin and trusted in Him, simply await the time when Christ will "redeem" us as His purchased possession, taking us to be with Him for all eternity to come.

My earnest prayer is that you, the reader, will claim this glorious offer of God's Loving Grace. Accept the offer of eternal life which comes only through Jesus Christ. He is the Way, the Truth, and the Life.

FIFTEEN

The Parable of the Pearl of Great Price

"The Kingdom of Heaven is like a merchant man seeking fine pearls." (Matthew 13:45-46)

In this parable, the Lord Jesus Christ emphasizes the nature and value of His True Church, being His own Spiritual Body of believers in this world. Again, we see at least two different interpretations commonly given of this parable. Of course, only one interpretation can be the truth. One interpretation erroneously identifies the merchant man as being the human here on this earth discovering the "pearl" of salvation. When the man discovered the "pearl of great price" he sold all he had in order to buy it. In truth, salvation cannot be purchased at any price. There is nothing we can pay, and nothing we can do in order to buy or earn true salvation.

In truth, the "merchant man" represents the Lord Jesus Christ. The "fine pearl" represents His Church in this world. Selling all that he has represents the fact that Jesus indeed paid all that He had with His own life, in order to pay the supreme price for His sacred Church, or "pearl."

The formation of the true Church, as the true Body of Christ, has covered a very large part of the mysteries of the Kingdom of Heaven, and is a mystery in itself. The Apostle Paul was given the insight and knowledge to explain this great mystery to anyone who will listen and understand it. In his writing in Romans 16:25-26, Paul explains: "Now to Him that has the power to establish you according to my gospel, and the preaching of Jesus Christ, according to the revelation of the mystery, which was kept secret since the world began, but is now made manifest (revealed), and by the scriptures of the prophets, according to the commandment of the everlasting God, made known to all nations for the obedience of faith."

The Apostle Paul continues to clarify and reveal the great mystery of the Church in this world (the "pearl of great price") in his writing to the Ephesians, Chapters 2 and 3. First, Paul tells us that each of us can become a part of the "building" or "habitation" of God through the Spirit. In other words, by your repentance of sin and your total faith in Jesus Christ as your Lord and Savior, you are born of the Spirit and become a part of the Spiritual Body of Christ and the "building" or "habitation" of God. Paul tells us that he serves Jesus Christ by revealing this great truth to us. Paul says that God revealed this great mystery of His Church to him as an Apostle for Jesus Christ, and he is going to share this mystery with us.

This mystery of the Church as the Body of Christ was not made known to the Old Testament prophets or faithful people, but was revealed to Christ's Holy Apostles and "prophets by the Spirit" (Ephesians 2:19 through 3:12). This great mystery is actually the fine pearl of Christ's parable and it is: "That the Gentiles (all people who are not Jewish in nationality) should be fellow heirs, and of the same Body, and partakers of God's promise in Christ by the Gospel, of which I was made a minister, according to the gift of the Grace of God given unto me by the effectual working of His power. Unto me, who am less than the least of all saints, is this grace given, that I should preach among the

Gentiles the unsearchable riches of Christ, and make all people see what is the fellowship of the mystery, which from the beginning of the world has been hidden in God, Who created all things by Jesus Christ, to the intent that now, unto the principalities and powers in heavenly places, might be known by the Church the manifold wisdom of God, according to the eternal purpose which He purposed in Christ Jesus, our Lord, in Whom we have boldness and access with confidence by the faith of Him." Paul's statement in Ephesians 5:32 clarifies even further: "This is a great mystery, but I speak concerning Christ and the Church."

Paul added even further explanation of this great mystery in his writing to the Colossians 1:24-27: Paul says, "I am a minister of the Gospel of Jesus Christ and I "now rejoice in my sufferings for you, and put behind me the punishment I suffered for Christ in my flesh for His Body's sake, which is the Church, of which I am made a minister, according to the dispensation of God which is given to me for you, to fulfill the Word of God, even the mystery which has been hidden from ages and from generations, but now is made manifest (revealed) to His saints, to whom God would make known what is the riches of the glory of this mystery among the Gentiles, which is ***Christ in you, the hope of glory.***"

C.I. Scofield gives us great insight in his notes from the Scofield Study Bible: "A pearl is an illustration of the Church: (1) A pearl is formed by accretion, and that not mechanically but vitally, as Christ adds to the Church. (2) Christ, having given Himself for the pearl, is now preparing it for presentation to Himself (Ephesians 5:25-27). The Kingdom is not just the Church, but the true children of the Kingdom during the fulfillment of these mysteries, baptized by one Spirit into one Body, compose the Church, the pearl" (1 Corinthians 12:12-13).

What makes this great mystery the "pearl of great price" is the fact that, when you are born of the Spirit by faith in Jesus Christ, not only do you become a part of His Body (His Church), but also, Jesus Christ comes to reside in you Spiritually. In the form of His Holy Spirit, Jesus Christ comes to be within you as you live your life here on earth awaiting your glorious transformation to your place in Heaven for all eternity. We know this as the "Baptism of the Spirit", which is what makes one a true child of God.

I am constantly amazed at my position in Christ as a part of His Body and at the presence of Christ within my life by His Holy Spirit. I realize that I am His "pearl of great price" because I am a part of His sacred Church. You can enjoy that same position and identity when you repent of the sin in your life and trust in Jesus Christ as your Lord and Savior.

SIXTEEN

The Parable of the Net

"The Kingdom of Heaven is like a net that was cast into the sea, and gathered of every kind." (Matthew 13:47-51)

This parable also describes the likeness of the Kingdom of Heaven from the viewpoint of God and His Spiritual presence in this world. Similar to the parable of the tares and wheat, this parable reveals the Spiritual Truth that God is "casting His net into the sea", representing the all-encompassing power of God to include every person who is ever born in His Sovereign and Holy plan for all of mankind and this world. Every single person ever born is under God's power and authority. Even those people who reject the very existence of God are under His Sovereign power and authority, whether they like it or not, or admit it or not. Remember, nothing changes the Truth of God.

In this parable, the Lord God Almighty is the One that casts His net into the earth. Every kind and sort of human being will be caught in God's great "net." Atheists, heathens, evil people, and people who think they are good, will be included in God's net, along with those people who are truly born-again children of God. As this parable states: "the Kingdom of Heaven is like a net, that was cast into the sea, and gathered of every kind, which, when it was full, they drew to shore, and sat down, and gathered the good into vessels, but cast the bad away. So shall it be at the end of the age (world). The angels shall come forth, and separate the wicked from among the righteous, and shall cast them (the wicked) into the furnace of fire; there shall be wailing and gnashing of teeth" (Matthew 13:47-50).

"When the net is full" refers to the "fullness of time" when God will declare this age of the world at an end. When the "net is full", the Lord Jesus Christ will come back to this earth in power and great glory, and will reign supreme over all the earth and the universe. At that time, "every knee will bow and every tongue will confess that Jesus Christ is Lord, to the glory of God, the Father" (Philippians 2:9-11), The "fullness of time" will come when the last person to become a member of the family of God, and a member of the Body of Christ is brought into the Kingdom. When this last person comes into the sacred and glorious Kingdom of God, all time as we know it will end. Then will come the Great White Throne Judgment where the wicked dead will be judged according to their rejection of Jesus Christ and God's Loving Grace and Salvation. (See Revelation 20:11-15).

The ones that will draw the "net" to shore will be those angels empowered by God to draw the net in and to separate the good from the bad, or the "wicked from among the righteous." The Lord Jesus Christ has the power of God over the angels and over judgment of this world. God alone works through His Divine Trinity to bring a final end to sin and evil in this world. Jesus Christ is the King and will judge all. Jesus will judge His own at the Judgment Seat of Christ, according to the works we have done in our life as a true Christian and child of God. Jesus, as the power of God will judge those who have never been born again of the Spirit at the Great White Throne Judgment. Those being judged at the Great White Throne Judgment will be those "wicked fish" caught up in God's great net.

They will be separated just like the goats will be separated from the sheep (See Matthew 25:32) and they will be cast into the burning, anguishing hell and finally, the Lake of Fire, where they will suffer forever. Just as Christ warns in this parable: "there will be wailing and gnashing of teeth."

At the great and final day God will separate and judge all people! The great preacher and man of God, W.A. Criswell, once related a story about when he was a young student in the seminary in Louisville. He went to a Baptist associational meeting in Indiana. There, he heard an old preacher with long white hair preach a sermon to the meeting. The preacher closed his sermon that day with the most poignant appeal for souls that young Criswell had ever heard. He said it went like this: "And we come to the casket, and our tears fall unbidden, and we say, 'Goodbye, sweet mother, goodbye,' or 'Goodbye, my darling son, goodbye,' or 'Goodbye, my precious child, goodbye.'" He said, "That's not 'goodbye'. I'll tell you what's 'goodbye'. At the great judgment of the Lord God Almighty, when the Lord has gathered us at the end of the age, and He separates us, like a shepherd divides the sheep from the goats or like the Lord God divides the fish in the net. Then, the wife will turn to the husband who never repented and trusted in Christ and say, 'Goodbye, husband. I'll never see you again,' or the mother will say to a rejecting and prodigal son, 'Goodbye, son. I'll never see you again.'" He said, "Now, that is 'goodbye.'"

This great "dragnet" of the Lord will be cast into the sea of humanity and will gather every kind of person, good and bad, saved and unsaved, carnal and Spiritual. These remain together in the net, just as in the world. The world will never be converted and saved in its evil and sinful state, so God will keep all of humanity in His "net" until He separates His own children from the rest of the world. In this world, (in God's net), God's children are not truly *of* the world. Just as Jesus stated in His intercessory prayer found in John, Chapter 17: "they are in the world, but not of the world."

Then, the Lord Jesus Christ asked the Apostles and other disciples He was teaching: "Have you understood all these things?" How critical it is that we listen carefully and intently enough that we can understand the meaning of God's teachings. "They said to Him, Yes, Lord." Here, Christ was asking about their understanding of each of the parables he shared with them during this period of teaching. The Lord is asking, "Do you understand each of these teachings?"

Do you truly understand these parabolic teachings of Jesus Christ? If you don't, you should realize that you may not be born again of

SEVENTEEN

The Parable of the Householder

"Every scribe who is instructed concerning the Kingdom of Heaven is like a man that is a householder, who brings forth out of his treasure things new and old." (Matthew 13:53)

This very short parable is almost an afterthought during this teaching by the Lord. Some people don't even consider this short parable when studying the other parables given here in the Thirteenth Chapter of Matthew. But, it is a parable nonetheless and should be considered a part of Christ's sacred teachings.

A "scribe" is literally any person who hears the message and teachings of Jesus Christ, opens and studies the Bible, and believes God's Word. In Mark 12:32-34 we see the account of a scribe who came to Jesus and asked Him; "Which is the first commandment of all?" (Mark 12:28). A scribe in the days of Jesus was a Jewish man who studied the Old Testament Scriptures and laws, writing them down for others to study and follow. Jesus answered him, giving the first great commandment of loving the Lord God with all you heart, soul, mind, and strength. Then, as He had done before, Jesus gave the scribe the second, and equal, commandment: "You shall love your neighbor as yourself." The scribe then repeated these commandments, adding that they were greater and more meaningful than "all whole burnt offerings and sacrifices." When Jesus saw that he had answered with intelligence and understanding, He said to the scribe: "You are not far from the Kingdom of God." And so, the scribe was not far, in knowledge, from the Kingdom of God, but he was not yet actually *within* the Kingdom of God. In order to be a true part of the Kingdom of God, the scribe, as well as any person, must also repent of sin and trust fully in Jesus Christ as Lord and Savior. Having the knowledge is not enough. We must each have the sincere repentance and love for Jesus Christ that leads to true Salvation and the Kingdom of God. It is not enough to have knowledge of the Bible. Many people have an intricate knowledge of the Bible but are not true children of God. It is not enough to have knowledge of the laws of God. You can be close, but not within the true Kingdom of God. This is what the Lord meant when He said, "you are not far from the Kingdom." I encounter people regularly who really enjoy debating and arguing over Scripture and the Bible. Many of these people are very intelligent and are very knowledgeable of the Bible. They often take great pride in being able to prove a point of contradiction or error in the Bible. Most of these people are very deluded and mistaken. They are not being Spiritual, but rather very worldly in their attitude. Jesus says that it is not enough to be knowledgeable. It is not enough to only believe that God exists or that Jesus Christ is real. Remember: **YOU MUST BE BORN AGAIN!** If a person is truly born again of the Spirit, then he or she will be concerned with the things of the Spirit, and not with things on the earth (Colossians 3:

In this parable, each and every person who is instructed in the Kingdom of Heaven, who studies and understands God's Word, and who trusts and believes in Jesus Christ as Lord is a "scribe." As a scribe, we become a "householder", or one who owns and inhabits our home within the Kingdom of Heaven. As a resident of the Kingdom of Heaven, we have great treasures given to us by God's Word and His Holy Spirit. We have the treasures of the teachings of Jesus Christ. We "bring forth" out of our treasure from both the Old Testament teachings of the Law of God, and the New Testament teachings of our Lord Jesus Christ.

We who are instructed in the faith of Jesus Christ, and we who know the Lord as our Savior and King, and God as our Heavenly Father, are to bring out things in our lives that are valuable to the Kingdom of God. We are to bring out things in our lives that will help to lead others to a saving knowledge of Jesus Christ as Savior.

The Lord is implying here that every true disciple of His is like a scribe. If you are a true Christian, then you have been told that, only by understanding God's Word can you bear good fruit in your life (Matthew 13:23). You are being asked if you truly understand all of these teachings. Understanding God's Word was a very fundamental aspect of being a scribe. Understanding God's Word is a very fundamental aspect of being a born-again child of God, and a true disciple of Jesus Christ. If you are a true disciple of Jesus Christ then you are expected to be like a scribe. The very word "disciple" means "learner", and implies that you are like a scribe.

Every true disciple of Jesus Christ is like a householder with a treasure. The treasure is the Word of God. The household is the true family of God, or the Kingdom of God. The greatest treasure of all is our Lord Jesus Christ and the salvation to eternal life that He gives us.

We have both old and new treasures. The Word of God contains both the Old Testament and the New Testament. Should we throw away an old treasure just because we have found a new one? The old treasure of the Old Testament only serves to help us appreciate the New Testament treasure even more. It is the revelation of the New Testament of Jesus Christ that helps us to understand the mysteries of the Old Testament as it prophesied of Christ. It was not until Jesus fulfilled the Old Law and explained the Old Testament prophecies that His disciples were able to understand more fully.

As a true disciple of Jesus Christ, I am richly blessed! I have been blessed to see and hear things that others did not in ancient days. I am blessed to see and hear things that many others do not in this day and time. I understand the parables and Christ's other teachings about the Kingdom of Heaven. I understand the prophecies of the Old

Testament. I possess the great treasures of God's Word in my life. I sincerely appreciate and love the great treasures God has given me. I appreciate most of all the treasure of Jesus Christ and the Salvation and eternal life that He gives me. Can you say this as well?

EIGHTEEN

The Parable of the Laborers

"The Kingdom of Heaven is like a man that is a householder, who went out early in the morning to hire laborers to work in his vineyard." (Matthew 20:1)

I would like to continue in the Lord's teachings regarding His Kingdom. There are other parables that the Lord presented in order to help us to understand the true meaning of the Kingdom of Heaven. Jesus used the common example of a householder, or resident landowner, hiring workers to do the work needed in his vineyard. Jesus doesn't explain the meaning of this parable to us so we must study and think about His words in order to fully understand His teaching. As we study this teaching together, I pray that God will reveal to each of us "the knowledge of the mysteries of the Kingdom of Heaven."

What is the Kingdom of Heaven like? "It is like a man that is a householder, who went out early in the morning (probably about 6:00 a.m.) to hire workers for his vineyard. And when he had agreed with the workers for a wage of one denarius (commonly a penny) a day, he sent them into his vineyard to work. And he went about the third hour (about 9:00 a.m.), and saw some other men who were standing idle in the marketplace. And he said to these men, 'Why don't you go work in my vineyard and whatever is a fair wage I will pay you'. And they went their way to work. Again, he went out about the sixth (about noon) and ninth hour (about 3:00 p.m.), and did the same thing, hiring other workers to go work in his vineyard. And about the eleventh hour (about 5:00 p.m.) he went out, and found others standing idle, and said to them, 'Why do you stand here all day not working'? And they answered him and said, 'Because we don't have anyone who will hire us'. So, he said to these men, 'Go also into my vineyard, and whatever is right and fair, I will pay you'. So when the evening came, the lord of the vineyard said to his steward (his foreman), 'Call the workers and give them their wages, beginning from the last ones hired to the first ones hired'. And when the men came who were hired at the eleventh hour, each man was paid a denarius (a full day's wage). But when the first men hired came, they supposed that they should have received more wages than those hired later; but they were likewise paid one denarius. And when they received their wages, they murmured and complained against the householder, saying, 'These last ones hired have only worked one hour, and you have made them equal to us by paying them the same wage, although we have worked hard in the heat all day long'. But the landowner answered one of them, and said, 'Friend, I don't do any wrong to you. Did you not agree to work all day for me for one denarius? Take your wages and go on your way; I will pay these last men hired the same as I am paying you. Is it not lawful for me to do as I please with my own money? Is your thought and attitude evil just because I am being good to other men'? So the last shall be first, and the first last; for many are called, but few are chosen."

This is one of the longer parables that Jesus taught. It seems that some of the disciples had shown a similar attitude of jealousy toward others who were receiving attention and love from the Lord. Jesus is teaching them a sacred and profound lesson.

The complaint of these workers in verses 11 and 12 reveals their true character. They had been dealt with very fairly, just as they had agreed, but they complained and protested when others had been dealt with generously.

The characters of this story are a landowner and his hired workers. The landowner's foreman is also mentioned. The setting is primarily relating to the vineyard, but also includes the surrounding area such as the marketplace, where men would gather and essentially loiter, since they did not have work. The landowner (householder) represents the Lord God. The workers represent those people who are saved by the loving Grace of God through faith and trust in the supreme sacrifice of Jesus Christ (true Christians). The vineyard represents the Kingdom of Heaven. The marketplace represents the world itself.

The foreman represents one who is chosen by God to serve in a special and very personal way. The work itself represents the Christian life, to be lived by every born-again child of God. Every Christian is a worker in the Kingdom of God.

This parable is teaching us that people out in the world are called by God to become His children. Everyone is offered salvation from hell, new birth of the Spirit, and eternal life in Heaven. God's loving Grace is offered to everyone, just as this landowner offered work to everyone he saw. Every person ever born is offered the opportunity to become a part of the Kingdom of God; a member of God's family; a joint heir with Jesus Christ. Not everyone accepts God's offer. Not every person accepts the offer to be a worker and earn wages.

Some people become Christians very early in life while some people may become a Christian on his/her death bed. The point of Christ's teaching is that, no matter the time of life, it is never too late to repent of sin and trust in Jesus as your Lord and Savior. The wages are the same for the long-time Christian and for the last-minute Christian. Remember the thief on the cross next to Jesus at His crucifixion? He showed a repentant heart and a true faith in Jesus as he asked the Lord to remember him when He came into His Kingdom. Jesus told him: "Today, you will be with me in paradise." He didn't work for the Lord like the Apostles did, yet he received the same glorious reward of Heaven.

On a personal note, I was born again and became a true child of God when I was nine years old. Ever since that remarkable moment I have dedicated myself to working for the Lord. At the age of sixteen I surrendered my life to God's service in any way He would use me.

I have faltered and failed along the way, but I have always come back to seeking God's absolute will and work for my life. I know fully well that some people have lived a very sinful and evil life for many years, and have realized at the last moments of their life that they are a lost sinner and bound for eternal hell and torment. As they repent and surrender themselves by faith to Jesus Christ, they become like the thief on the cross. They go on to be with the Lord in Heaven, even at that point. Am I jealous of that? Not in the least bit. As a matter of fact, I wouldn't trade my life of living with the Holy Spirit of God as my comforter and strength, and Jesus Christ as my Lord and Savior, for any amount of time in sin and the world. In fact, I continue to plead with people to surrender your life immediately to Christ and His Salvation. You are not promised another breath or another second of life in this world. You are going to die like all of us. You may not have the chance to be on a death bed.

You may die in an instant without even realizing your death. You may have a massive heart attack, or a tragic accident that kills you instantly. The time to go to work with the landowner of the vineyard is right now. The time to give your soul up to God by faith in Jesus Christ is right now.

Some of the people who have been serving God for many years of their life may resent those who live a sinful and evil life for the majority of their time, and come to Salvation at the very end or very late in life. It is certainly sad if they do resent it. The Kingdom of Heaven is not a business like the world's business. The Kingdom of Heaven is God's Spiritual business. That is why Christ used this example. Anyone hearing this story would say, "well, that's not good business to pay the same for one who has worked only one hour of the day the same as the one who has worked a full twelve hours. In fact, that's not good business. But the Kingdom of Heaven is like that. It is not like the business of the world. It is like the business of God. God is calling every person to repentance and to His gift of eternal life. It is never too late in life to accept His gift, and the rewards are the same for all: Eternal Life in the Kingdom of God.

Perhaps the key verse in this parable is Matthew 20:16. Jesus used the phrase: "the last shall be first, and the first last." We should notice in Matthew 19:30 that Jesus said: "many that are first shall be last, and the last shall be first." This phrase serves to teach us that, if we consider ourselves to be "first", or better than others, we are really last, because of our attitude of arrogance and haughtiness. Christ teaches us to be humble and meek in every aspect of our life. We should actually strive to serve others while considering ourselves to be "last" in the world's point of view. In the Kingdom of Heaven, when we put ourselves "last", we are actually "first" in the sight of our Heavenly Father.

The last part of this verse states: "For many are called, but few are chosen." Over the years, I have had several people ask me to explain what this statement really means. Christ has really emphasized this statement in His teachings because He used it again as the last statement of His parable of the Marriage Feast in Matthew 22:1-14. In fact, this statement can be considered a summary of what the Kingdom of Heaven will be like at the end of the age. This statement teaches us that God calls every person ever born to repent of sin and trust in Jesus Christ as Lord. In fact, we know from Peter's teaching in 2 Peter 3:9 that: "The Lord is not slack concerning His promise, as some people consider slackness, but is longsuffering toward us, not willing that any should perish, but that all should come to repentance." It is part of God's Sovereign Truth that He offers every single person eternal life, if the person is simply willing to repent of sin and trust by faith in Jesus Christ as Lord of their life. The "many" of this statement actually includes "all".

But, the sad truth is: every person will not listen to God and accept His offer of salvation and eternal life. Only the person who sincerely repents of sin and trusts in Jesus Christ as Lord and Savior will be among the "chosen" throughout all eternity. When the end of the age comes, there will only be a few chosen from among the "many" who were called.

What does this parable teach those who are willing to listen, understand, and believe? It teaches us that God is loving and generous with every person living. He gives each person willing to accept it His Grace.

And what is Grace? Grace is giving us something we don't deserve. God's *justice* would give us what we deserve: Death and hell as our punishment. God's *mercy* does not give us what we deserve. God spares us the torment and punishment of hell and declares us "Not Guilty!" God's *Grace* gives us what we don't deserve: Heaven and eternal life with Him.

What does this parable teach us about the Kingdom of Heaven? It tells us that God's Kingdom does not operate on the same principles as business in this world. God's Kingdom is not an earthly kingdom. It is God's Spiritual Kingdom and is offered to all at every moment in life.

This parable teaches us that we can be a part of God's Kingdom by His Grace. We cannot earn it by working. We cannot have enough money to buy it. Jesus Christ paid the full and complete price for all sin. No one can be a part of God's Kingdom except through Jesus Christ. Christ said: "I am the Way, the Truth, and the Life. No one comes to the Father except by Me."

NINETEEN

The Parables of the Two Sons, the Householder, and the Wedding Feast (Matthew 21:28 - 22:14)

"For many are called, but few are chosen." (Matthew 22:14)

You may be wondering: What do these parables teach us about the Kingdom of God? They seem to be parables about the value of making the right decisions for service to the Lord. Well, just as with all the other parables and teachings of Jesus Christ, the lessons to be learned relate directly to the true meaning of the Kingdom of Heaven.

These three parables are closely related because Christ taught them almost together during the brief time between His triumphal entry into Jerusalem at the Passover time, and His Crucifixion. These three parables are found in Matthew's Gospel, but the Parable of the Householder is also given in the Gospel accounts of Mark and Luke (Mark 12:1-9; Luke 20:9-19), while the Parable of the Wedding Feast is also found in Luke's Gospel (Luke 14:16-24).

In each of these parabolic teachings, the Lord Jesus Christ is teaching us further just what the Kingdom of Heaven is like by showing us just what kind of people will **not** be a part of the Kingdom. Christ makes it very clear to us that, not only murderers, thieves, and evil acting people will not see the Kingdom of Heaven, but also missing the Kingdom will be those people who "act religious" but who do not have a true love for Jesus Christ and who have never actually repented of sin and trusted fully in Jesus Christ as Lord and Savior. These are the seemingly "good" people of our society who really think they are okay for eternity, but truly have no part of the Kingdom of God. These will be the people to whom the Lord will speak the fateful words: "Depart from Me, I never knew you."

As with the Lord's other teachings, we should be careful to consider the audience to whom Jesus is speaking. We should always consider the overall context of the Lord's message in order to clearly understand it. The account given to us in Chapters 21 and 22 of Matthew's Gospel begins with Christ's triumphal entry into Jerusalem during the time of Passover. The crowd around the Lord is responding to Him by shouting praises and spreading palm branches and articles of clothing before Him as a gesture of worship and praise (Matthew 21:8-9). The Lord's first act when entering Jerusalem is to cleanse the Temple from the dishonest "moneychangers". The Lord then proceeded to heal the blind and the lame, while reinforcing the true purpose of the Temple (Matthew 21:12-17).

At this time we see the response of the religious leaders of the Jewish people (Matthew 21:15). The chief priests and the scribes were very displeased when they saw the people respond in worship and praise to Jesus. In fact, these religious leaders were showing their true inner feelings. While they worshipped God physically with words and practices, their true heart and inner soul was not faithful to God. They were hypocrites, and Jesus was going to respond to them for what they were.

After His departure from the Temple, He left the city for the night, and returned the next morning. We then see Jesus cursing a fig tree for having full branches and leaves, but not bearing fruit (Matthew 21:18-22.

With this action, the Lord is teaching us that, having outward appearance of faith and love for God is not enough in our lives. We must be truly dedicated to God and faithful to Him in our very inner being. By loving God and being faithful and trusting to Jesus Christ we show the true "fruit" of the Spirit in our lives. Our service to the Lord is genuine and faithful, repenting of sin and turning away from the evil of the world. The fig tree is often used as being symbolic of Israel (Hosea 9:10; Joel 1:7). The fact that the fig tree had leaves but no fruit is symbolic of Israel's religious activity, but no substance of faith and love for God. Israel, as represented by their religious leaders, had the "leaves" of activity, but not the "fruit" of repentance and obedience to God. This is precisely why Jesus tells them that "the publicans (dishonest tax collectors) and the harlots (prostitutes) will enter the Kingdom of God before you" (Matthew 21:31).

In Matthew 21:23-27, the religious leaders of chief priests and elders question Jesus' authority. Who is this Jesus who comes into Jerusalem receiving the praises of all the people, and then drives the moneychangers out of the Temple? Just who does this Jesus think he is? This chain of events sets the stage for a very serious and profound time of teaching and clarification by the Lord Jesus Christ. The Lord does not avoid the confrontation or the truth with these hypocritical people. It is in this context that Jesus shares the three parables we examine here: The Two Sons, The Householder, and The Wedding Feast. Each of these parables is directed to the Jewish religious leaders, while giving the entire world the Truth of God through the teachings of Jesus Christ. Each parable illustrates the religious Israel's rejection of Jesus Christ as the True Messiah and Savior of the world. Each parable pronounces judgment on Israel for their rejection of Christ as their promised Messiah.

Parable of the Two Sons

The basic story in the first parable is of a man with two sons who told each of the sons to go to work in the vineyard. The first son refused, but later changed his mind and went to work, finally obeying his father. The second son initially agreed to go to work but actually disobeyed his father by not actually following through with his verbal commitment.

So, in this first parable of the two sons, the leaders of Israel are the second son who claimed obedience, but did not do the will of the father. Even the dishonest and sinful people of this world who repent of sin and trust in Jesus Christ as Lord and Savior will go into the Kingdom of God before these hypocritical religious people.

Jesus is telling the priests and religious leaders that they have claimed to accept the will and message from God but they have failed to live up to it by being disobedient. Outwardly they are pious and appear to be people of God, but God knows their true heart and they have failed Him totally.

Jesus is speaking to all people who never truly repent of sin and trust totally in Him as Lord of his or her life. There are multitudes of people in our world who are "good" people according to our social human standards, but who either ignore God's direct command to repent and trust in Christ, or reject the concept of salvation and new birth of the Spirit altogether.

These are the people who will join the truly evil people of the world, along with Satan and his demons, and will spend all eternity in Hell and the Lake of Fire, never knowing any part of the Kingdom of God.

The first son, however, is the person who has truly "repented" of the wrong he or she has done in life by disobeying God. In Matthew 21:29 we see the first son answering his father and saying initially; "I will not: but afterward repented, and went." The term *repented* truly describes what Christ is teaching. Unless you are willing to genuinely and sincerely repent of the sin in your life and turn to Jesus by faith as your Lord, then you will never see the Kingdom of Heaven.

Of course, the father in this parable represents God. God is telling every person who ever lives to repent of sin and trust in Jesus Christ in order to be born of the Spirit and enjoy the true Spiritual relationship as a child of God. Then God tells each of us to go out into the "vineyard" of the world and share His Gospel of Salvation with others who are lost and without Jesus as Lord. This "work" is what Jesus means by the sons "going to work in the vineyard."

In Matthew 21:32 Jesus declares to the religious acting people that "John (the Baptist) came unto you in the way of righteousness, and you did not believe him: but the tax collectors and prostitutes (outward sinners) believed him: and you, when you had seen it, did not repent afterward, so that you might believe him." Jesus is saying that all hypocrites who do not have a truly repentant heart and faith in Jesus Christ as Lord will not have a part of the Kingdom of God.

Parable of the Householder

This parable appears in three of the Gospel accounts in the Bible, with Matthew's account being the most complete. However, there are some additions in the other accounts that make it most valuable to study all three accounts so as to have the greatest understanding of Christ's teaching here. This parable follows the Parable of the Two Sons immediately and is Christ's efforts to help them to truly understand His Truth. Not only is Christ teaching these false religious leaders, but He is also teaching anyone who is willing to listen and understand His Truth.

In order to get the true context given here, we need to look first at Matthew 21:18. Jesus goes to the temple court early in the morning to teach (Matthew 21:23). While He is teaching, the chief priests and elders of the Jewish religious sect confront Him, wanting to know by what authority He is teaching. Jesus, as in many instances during His ministry of teaching, does not allow them to control the conversation or the moment. Jesus answers their question by asking them a question (Matthew 21:24-26). Of course, the religious leaders don't like Christ's question or His response to their answers. In effect, Jesus tells them that they will not succeed in their attempt to rebuke or humiliate Him, and therefore, He is not obligated to answer their questions (Matthew 21:27).

What Jesus tells them is that both He and John the Baptist received their authority from the same source (directly from God).

This incident causes the religious leaders to become very angry and puts them in severe opposition to Jesus. Jesus then frustrates them even further by telling the Parable of the Two Sons and this Parable of the Householder (also known as the Parable of the Vineyard or the Wicked Tenants).

In our study of this parable, we need to consider the six main characters included by Jesus, and the actual subject that each represents:

1. The Landowner (Householder) – God
2. The Vineyard – the Nation of Israel
3. The Tenants (Farmers or Husbandmen) – the Jewish religious leaders
4. The Landowner's Servants – the Prophets of old who were obedient to God's Will and command to preach His Word to the people of Israel
5. The Son – Jesus Christ
6. The Other Tenants – the Gentiles of the world

(For further enlightenment it would be beneficial to also study the parable given by the Prophet Isaiah, in Isaiah Chapter 5).

Additionally, the "hedge" and the "tower" were built for the vineyard and are symbolic of what God has done for the Nation of Israel to watch over and protect it. The "winepress" was dug in the vineyard as being symbolic of the harvest, when the winepress was used to press the grapes to make the wine. As was the custom of the time, the landowner, being absent and leaving the vineyard to be managed by the tenant farmers (husbandmen), would expect as much as half of the grapes (or finished wine) as payment by the tenants for the use of his land.

In Matthew 21:34-36, Jesus tells us that the landowner (householder) sent his servants to collect his portion of the harvest and how they were cruelly mistreated by the tenant farmers (husbandmen). Some of the servants were beaten, some were stoned, and some were even killed. The householder then sent even more of his servants a second time and they received the same treatment. As we see in the characterizations, the servants represent the prophets God has sent to His people (Israel), only to have them rejected, beaten, stoned, and killed by the very people who were claiming to be obedient and faithful to God. The Prophet Jeremiah was beaten (Jeremiah 26:7-11), John the Baptist was killed (Matthew 14:1-12), and others were stoned (2 Chronicles 24:21). In this parable Jesus is not only reminding the religious leaders what they were really like, but He was posing to them a crucial question: How could they claim to be obedient and faithful to God and still reject His messengers and teachers? Throughout history, God has repeated His appeal to people through His prophets and preachers to the unrepentant people of both Israel and the world in general.

In Matthew 21:37-39, the situation during this parable account becomes even more critical. The landowner now sends his own son to the tenant farmers, believing that they will surely respect him. But not only do the tenants reject the son, they actually believe that, if they kill the son, they will receive his inheritance. At that time, the law provided that if there were no living heirs to a property then the property would pass to those in actual possession. In fact, Christ is telling these religious leaders that they are not only rejecting Him as the One True Son of God, but that they are actually going to kill Him out of their hatred and sinfulness (see Psalm 118:22 and Isaiah 28:16). As we see in Acts 4:8-12, the Apostle Peter would make the same charges against the religious establishment of the time. The tenants in the parable then thought that their actions would end their fight for the property, but they would be wrong again.

Jesus Christ now asks the critical question in Matthew 21:40: "When the lord of the vineyard comes back, what will he do to these husbandmen?" To clarify in true meaning: "What will God finally do to those who ignore or reject Jesus Christ?" Please always keep in mind that ignoring Jesus Christ is the same as rejecting Him. No decision made in life is a NO decision for salvation.

What Jesus is doing is forcing the religious leaders to acknowledge their own fate for eternity. He is forcing them to realize their fate of condemnation and eternal separation from God for their disobedience and hypocrisy.

In Matthew 21:42 Jesus turns from dealing with the immediate situation of Israel and its past disobedience to God and turns to the point of what Israel and its religious leadership is going to do with Him as the True Messiah, the Son of God, whom He refers to as "the chief cornerstone." Cornerstones and capstones are used symbolically in Scripture and here symbolizes Christ as the main piece of the foundation of the True Church in the world. Christ is the main foundation for all those who come to be a true member of the Lord's Church and true member of the Family of God, being a true part of the Kingdom of God. The prophecy of Psalm 118:22-23 is declared to be true as Jesus is to be rejected by the religious establishment and ultimately crucified.

Perhaps the very key to understanding this parable is found in Matthew 21:43. Jesus declares very directly that "the Kingdom of God shall be taken from you, and given to a nation that will bring out the very fruits of the Kingdom." Jesus is declaring that the Kingdom of Heaven will not be available to these hypocritical sinners as God has offered, but will be made available to the rest of the world, and anyone repenting of sin and trusting fully in Jesus Christ as Lord will receive the Kingdom of Heaven as their eternal reward. The Kingdom of God will be given to anyone willing to confess and repent of sin and trust in Jesus Christ.

One preacher and teacher of God's Word put it this way: "there will be a new people of God made up of all peoples who will temporarily replace the Jews so that Jesus can establish His Church. This will change the way God deals with man, from the old dispensation of the law to a new dispensation of God's grace. It will usher in a period of time where man will no longer understand forgiveness of sins as man's work through what he does or doesn't do or by the sacrifices of animals on the altar, but by the work of Christ on the Cross. It will be a time where each individual can have a personal and saving relationship with the One and only God of the universe."

Jesus spoke of those who would "produce fruit", meaning the

authority given to the True Church to share the Gospel of Jesus Christ to the lost people of the world. Up to this time, the Jews felt that they had automatic membership in God's Kingdom because of their relationship to Abraham. But the new people of God would truly have what God wanted for Israel all along: a personal, sacred, and holy relationship that would be honored by God through the spreading of His Holy Word to all peoples.

Jesus continues His reference to the cornerstone in Matthew 21:44 to show how a stone can be used to build something beautiful, such as His Church, or it can be used to crush and destroy, depending on how the person treats it. This reference is likened to God's Word.

To some people, God's Word is salvation and eternal life. To others, God's Word is foolish and troublesome because it convicts people of their sins (2 Timothy 3:16). God's Word **is** Jesus Christ, and He is the way to salvation and eternal life of peace and joy, or He is the great Judge Who will declare the casting away of those rejecting Him to eternal suffering and separation in Hell and the Lake of Fire.

As Christ revealed Himself as the "chief cornerstone" He was revealing Himself to the Nation of Israel, coming to them, not in the glory and power of a great earthly king, but in humility, as a servant. He is revealed further in Scripture as a Stumbling Stone and Rock of offense as He convicts people of their sin of disobedience to God (see Isaiah 8:14-15; Romans 9:32-33; 1 Corinthians 1:23; 1 Peter 2:8). Jesus was also revealing Himself to His True Church, as He serves as the Foundation Stone and the Head of the Corner. This is Christ's reference to Himself in a Spiritual sense (see also 1 Corinthians 3:11; Ephesians 2:20-22; 1 Peter 4:5). Also, Christ was revealing Himself to the Gentile world as the Spiritual "Smiting Stone" which would crush the evil nature of this sinful world (see Daniel 2:34). Spiritually speaking, Israel "stumbled over" Christ, the Church is built upon Christ, and Gentile world dominion, led by Satan, will be crushed by Christ (see Revelation 16:13-16 and 19:17).

Finally, Matthew 21:45-46 gives us insight into the inner thoughts of the chief priests and leaders of the religious establishment of Israel. They were very jealous and envious of the popularity Jesus had with the public or common people. Christ's popularity encroached on their own authority and power to govern the people. These religious leaders have come to the realization that Jesus is actually talking about them and this infuriates them. They are embarrassed in front of the people. They understood the analogy Jesus used with the son, referring to Himself. This was blasphemous to them, and they would now try to kill Jesus, but waited to plan further, out of fear of the crowds.

From this point forward, the Jewish leaders would meet in secrecy to plot how they would get rid of Jesus. They were very secretive because of Christ's popularity. The people saw Jesus as a great prophet from God, and arresting Him or hurting Him publicly would cause a rebellious uprising, and compromise their relationship with Roman authorities.

As for any parable, you and I should apply the true meaning to our own lives. First of all, have you come to know Jesus Christ as your Lord and Savior, or have you ignored and rejected Him like the Jewish leadership did? The way by which you can come to know Christ as Lord and Savior is to admit your sinful condition, repent and turn away from your sins, and trust in Christ as the only way by which you are forgiven. You will then be born of the Spirit and become a true child of God and heir to the Kingdom. And secondly, if you are a true believer in Jesus Christ, ask yourself this question: What have you done with Jesus? Are you truly living for Him, or are you continuing to live like the world. What are you doing with the "gifts" of life and ability He has given you? What are you doing with your physical talents? What are you doing with your time? What are you doing with your money? What you do with these things in your life reflects your true relationship with God. Study God's Word diligently and pray for His guidance and wisdom in your life. Seek His Will for your life and live it day by day.

Parable of the Wedding Feast

In this last parable of Christ's "trilogy" of teachings directed to the sinful religious hypocrites of the Jewish people, as well as to all people everywhere who will listen and learn the Truth of God, the Lord clarifies what the Kingdom of God is like. Anyone who is to be a part of the Kingdom of Heaven must be a part of the Kingdom of God. Hopefully, you are beginning to understand the unity and dynamics of God's True Kingdom.

Knowing that these pious, arrogant and hypocritical religious leaders were not really understanding what He was teaching, Jesus went one step further to explain the Truth to them. In Matthew 22:1-14 we receive one more profound and sacred teaching from the Lord. This is known as the Parable of the Wedding Feast, or the Parable of the Marriage Feast. In many ways it is very similar to the Parable of the Great Banquet found in the Gospel of Luke, 14:15-24. The occasions given in the two parables are a little different and there are some other differences as well, but the meaning is the same. In order to better understand the Lord's teaching it is again important to consider the context and some basic facts regarding these types of ceremonies in the day Christ was teaching.

In Jewish society, the parents of the bride and groom generally created a marriage contract. The bride and groom would meet (in some cases for the first time) to sign this contract and make it binding. The couple was actually considered to be married at this point, but they would separate until the time of the actual ceremony. After the groom had prepared a home for them, he would return for his bride and the marriage ceremony and the wedding banquet would take place. How remarkably similar is this occasion to the Truth of God as He gives each person who repents of sin and trusts in Christ a new Spirit in which we become a part of the Body of Christ and a part of His Bride, the Church. When we become a born-again child of God, we are "betrothed" to Christ as part of His Church. Jesus has gone to prepare a place for us, and will come again to take us to the great "Marriage Supper of the Lamb", where we will be a Spiritual "Bride of Christ" (Revelation 19:9).

The wedding banquet was one of the most joyous occasions in Jewish life and could last for up to a week. In this parable, Jesus compares Heaven to a wedding feast that a king had prepared for his son (Matthew 22:2). Many people had been invited, but when the time for the banquet came, those invited refused to come (Matthew 22:4-5). In fact, the servants who were sent by the king to invite the guests were actually beaten and even killed by those who had been invited (Matthew 22:6).

The king became very angry with those who had been invited and did not come to the feast and sent his army to punish those who had beaten and killed his servants (Matthew 22:7). The king then sent invitations to anyone his servants could find in the world. The servants went out and invited both good and bad people to the wedding feast, and the banquet hall was filled with people (Matthew 22:8-10).

During the feast we see that the king noticed a man "who was not wearing the wedding clothes" (Matthew 22:11-12). In those days, it would be an insult to the king not to wear the garment provided to the guests for the feast.

When the man was asked how he was there and not properly clothed for the feast, he had no answer. The king ordered the man evicted from the banquet, "bound hand and foot, and thrown outside" (Matthew 22:13). Jesus also stated that the man who was not supposed to be at the wedding feast was to be thrown out into the outer darkness, "where there would be weeping and gnashing of teeth" (Matthew 22:13). Quite literally, those people who will not be acceptable for the great Wedding Feast of the Lord Jesus Christ will be cast away into the outer darkness of Hell and finally into the Lake of Fire. There will literally be excruciating wailing and weeping and gnashing of teeth.

Jesus then ends His teaching with the profound statement: "For many are called, but few are chosen" (Matthew 22:14). As I mentioned earlier in this writing, I have been asked on several occasions just what Jesus meant by this statement. It bears repeating. The Lord also made this statement in His teaching of the Parable of the Laborers found in Matthew 20:1-16. This parable clarifies the Lord's statement very well. Many people in this world, including the Nation of Israel, have been called by God to be a part of His Kingdom. In other words, many people hear the call of God to repentance and salvation, but only a few truly heed His call. In fact, each and every person ever born is called to repentance and faith in Jesus Christ. As we see in 1 Peter 3:9, God is "not willing that any should perish, but that all should come to repentance." The call by God to all people is the invitation to the great Wedding Feast, or Marriage Supper of the Lamb. Only those who are wearing the white robes representing their Spiritual birth and union with Christ will be accepted at the feast. The proper wedding garment for the Marriage Feast of the Lamb is provided by Jesus Christ and is put on us by the righteousness of Jesus Christ Himself. Unless we have it on us, we will miss the wedding feast. The man who was not wearing the proper clothing represents any person who does not wear the white robe of the Spirit. Many are called to repentance and trust in Christ, inviting each to be a part of the Bride of Christ, but few are actually chosen by repenting of sin and trusting fully in Christ as Lord and Savior, making each a cherished and honored guest at the Marriage Supper of the Lamb.

In this parable, the king is God the Father and the son being honored at the banquet is the Lord Jesus Christ, Who is indeed God the Son. John 1:11 tells us that Jesus Christ "came to that which was His own, but His own did not receive Him." Jesus Christ came to seek and to save all who are lost and in sin. Christ invites all to be a part of His great feast. Many will not accept Christ and will not attend the eternal feast of joy and peace in the Kingdom of Heaven.

The guests invited originally to come to the wedding feast represents the Nation of Israel, which actually had the personal invitation from God to His Kingdom. When the time came for the Kingdom of Heaven to appear on this earth (see Matthew 3:1), they refused to recognize Christ as Who He is, and refused God's invitation to the great wedding feast in eternity. Many prophets of old, as well as John the Baptist, had been murdered by the very people God sent them to invite to His Kingdom (Matthew 14:10). The king's vengeance upon those who killed his servants in this parable is representative of God's vengeance upon those who killed

His prophets. The destruction of Jerusalem in 70 A.D. is one example of God's punishment upon Israel.

Ultimately, God's vengeance will be carried out on all who reject Jesus Christ and His offer of forgiveness and salvation. There will be desolation brought upon this sinful world, as stated in the Book of Revelation. God is very patient toward the sinful people of the world. He hates sin but He loves the sinner. But, God will not tolerate wickedness and sin forever. His judgment will come upon those who reject His offer of salvation through Jesus Christ. And, considering the price Jesus Christ paid on the cruel Cross for this sin, the judgment of God is well deserved (Hebrews 10:29-31).

It is also very important to note that the guests originally invited to the wedding feast refused to come to the banquet. It is not a matter of not being able to come. Everyone had an excuse for not accepting the king's invitation. How similar it is to our world today. Most people have an excuse as to why they are ignoring or refusing God's invitation to salvation and eternal life in His Kingdom. How tragic and sad it is to see so many people living in either ignorance or total rejection of God and the sacrifice of Jesus Christ on the Cross just for them.

The invitation to the wedding feast is then extended to anyone and everyone, including total strangers, both good and bad. God is extending His invitation to anyone and everyone, including both good and bad in this world. This represents the Gospel of Salvation of Jesus Christ being taken to the entire Gentile world, instead of exclusively to the Jewish Nation of Israel. This part of Christ's parable is a prophecy and foretelling of the Jew's rejection of the Gospel we see in Acts, Chapter 13. Paul and Barnabas were in Antioch when the Jewish religious leaders strongly opposed them, rejecting the Gospel of Christ they were presenting. The king in the parable proclaimed that those who refused to come to the feast "did not deserve to come." Acts 13:46 tells us: "We had to speak the Word of God to you first. Since you reject it and do not show yourselves to be worthy of eternal life, we now turn to the Gentiles." Keep in mind that *Gentiles* are all people of the world who are not born as a Jew, or of the ancestral lineage of Israel.

To summarize this teaching by the Lord Jesus Christ, God sent His beloved Son into this world, and the very people who should have celebrated and declared His coming actually rejected Him. Their rejection brought God's judgment upon them. As a result, the Kingdom of Heaven was opened up to anyone and everyone who will put self-righteousness aside, repent of the sin that is a part of every life, and by pure faith accept Jesus Christ as the only sacrifice capable of providing the righteousness that God requires to be a part of His Kingdom. Those people who ignore or reject this free gift of forgiveness and salvation will spend eternity in Hell and the Lake of Fire.

The Pharisees and religious hypocrites who heard this parable didn't miss the point. They "got it." Matthew 22:15 tells us that they "went out and laid plans to trap Him in His words." This Parable of the Wedding Feast is a warning to all people, to make sure you are relying on Jesus Christ for your salvation and eternal life, and not on your own good works or religious activity. It is also our teaching of what the Kingdom of God, which contains the Kingdom of Heaven, is really like.

TWENTY

The Kingdom of Heaven Summary

"Fear not, little flock; for it is your Father's good pleasure to give you the Kingdom." (Luke 12:32)

The general and paramount theme of the teachings of Jesus Christ is "The Kingdom of Heaven." Many, if not most, of the parables of Christ begin with, or include, "the Kingdom of Heaven is like . . ." (Matthew 13:24, 31, 33, 44, 45, 47). The Kingdom of Heaven was the main theme of the Lord's ministry while here on the earth and was included as the primary focal point of His Sermon on the Mount (Matthew 4:17, 23; Matthew 5:3-10, 19-20; Matthew 6:10, 33; Matthew 7:21).

As we have seen from our study in the preceding chapters of this text, the terms "Kingdom of Heaven" and "Kingdom of God" are primarily interchangeable but present a few noticeable distinctions. As I stated earlier, the terms have the similar distinction, spiritually, as the terms God the Father, God the Son, and God the Holy Spirit. Each is one in the same Divine Trinity, yet serving a particular and specific purpose in God's Sovereign Plan. After all, why would Scriptural writers choose to use the different expressions if there was no difference. In fact, we find that Matthew used the expression "Kingdom of Heaven" almost exclusively, while the other Gospel writers used the phrase "Kingdom of God." It has been suggested by some theologians that Matthew wrote his Gospel account to the Jews and chose to use the term "Kingdom of Heaven." The Jews were reluctant to use the Name of God out of reverence and sanctity. It is also suggested that the Jews had a great misconception of the coming "kingdom", anticipating a physical and earthly kingdom, while the term "heaven" would describe a spiritual kingdom, hopefully clarifying the Lord's teaching as being Spiritual in nature instead of physical.

We have seen that the true Kingdom of God includes the entire universe and all of eternal time: past, present, and future. God, in His Sovereign Will and purpose, chose to send down His Kingdom to the earth. God sent His Kingdom in the form and Person of Jesus Christ, His eternal and Divine Son. Jesus embodied the Kingdom of Heaven, which was, and is, included as a part of the eternal Kingdom of God. In a sense, we can discern the Kingdom of Heaven as being the Spiritual realm which includes all of the people who repent of sin and trust by faith in Jesus Christ as Lord. While we true believers are still here on this earth, we are a part of the Lord's spiritual Kingdom of Heaven. Additionally, we have become a part of the eternal Kingdom of God and will enjoy our eternal presence and existence in God's eternal Kingdom throughout all eternity future.

The term "kingdom" has historically been used to describe the concept of "reign" or "dominion", while also describing the geographical region under the reign of the ruler or magistrate of the kingdom. One example is the United Kingdom that we know as England or Great Britain. This kingdom has historically been ruled by a king or queen and includes specific geographic boundaries. Jesus used the term to describe a Spiritual Kingdom created and ruled over by God Almighty. The Kingdom of God described by Jesus Christ is the Spiritual Kingdom that includes all of God's creation for all eternity in time.

Therefore, the Kingdom of God, or Kingdom of Heaven is wherever God chooses it to be, whether in Heaven, where God dwells, or here on earth, where Jesus Christ came to bring salvation to the lost. In the true sense, the Kingdom of God has always existed but was presented to mankind on this earth in the form of the Lord Jesus Christ. The prophet Daniel foretold of the coming of the Kingdom in Daniel 2:44-45. The New Testament prophet John the Baptist proclaimed the Kingdom as being with us in Matthew 3:1-3. Jesus Christ preached and taught of the Kingdom in His earthly ministry and it is through Jesus Christ that the true Kingdom of God is realized in our world today (see also 1 Corinthians 15:23-26; Ephesians 1:20-22; 1 Peter 3:22; Revelation 1:5).

So, the Kingdom of God includes the Kingdom of Heaven and describes the reign of God over His entire universe, being Spiritual in nature. God's Kingdom shows itself to human beings in Spiritual ways (John 18:36; Romans 14:17). The people who choose to believe God's Word, repent of sin, and trust by faith in Jesus Christ as Lord then become the "Body" making up the Kingdom of Heaven, which is visibly manifested in the world in the form of the True Church: the Church as the Body of Christ.

The True Church is a community of human souls that have been born of the Spirit of God, who serve the One True God as Sovereign and Holy, making the Church the actual Kingdom of God in the world today. In effect, the terms "Kingdom" and "Church" can also be used somewhat interchangeably, with each serving a distinct purpose in God's Sovereign Plan.

And so, the Kingdom of Heaven has both an eternal future characteristic as well as a present element in today's world. The future element is spoken of by Jesus in Matthew 25:34, by Paul in 1 Corinthians 15:50 and 2 Timothy 4:18, and by Peter in 2 Peter 1:10-11. Peter also referred to the future eternal element of the Kingdom in 2 Peter 3:10-13, helping us to understand that the Kingdom of Heaven involves the "new heavens and new earth" to be put in place by God for all eternity.

In the past tense, the Kingdom of God has always existed and has had God almighty as the Sovereign power and authority. God has always included His Son, Jesus Christ, and his Holy Spirit in His Kingdom reign as well (see John 2:1-5).

In the present tense, the Kingdom of God is found wherever

the Sovereignty of God is accepted in the lives of men and women. Presently, the Kingdom of Heaven is a Spiritual Kingdom, without any geographical boundaries or physical elements. The Kingdom of Heaven is manifested in the True Church in our world today. The Kingdom of Heaven was brought to earth in the embodiment of Jesus Christ and was expressed Spiritually on the Day of Pentecost as recorded in Acts, Chapter 2.

In the future tense, the Kingdom of Heaven will be brought to fruition with the coming of the Lord Jesus Christ to earth the second time in "power and great glory." The Lord Jesus Christ will then deliver the Kingdom of God to the Father as recorded in 1 Corinthians 15:24. When Christ comes triumphantly, "then the righteous will shine forth as the sun in the Kingdom of their Father" (Matthew 13:43). The Kingdom will then be that "new heavens and new earth" described by Peter and John "in which righteousness dwells" (2 Peter 3:13). And in the future Kingdom we will see that the "tabernacle of God is with men, and He will dwell with them, and they shall be His people, and God Himself will be with them and be their God" (Revelations 21:3).

Finally, the Kingdom of God will be experienced only by those people who are a part of the Body of Christ; the True Church, brought together as the Bride of Christ at the great feast and Marriage Supper of the Lamb of God. These are the people who are repentant of their sin and who trust by faith in Jesus Christ alone as the means by which they can be saved. These are the people who are "diligent to be found by Him in peace" (2 Peter 3:13-15). These are the people who do "the will of my Father in Heaven" (Matthew 7:21-23).

"Thy Kingdom come, Thy Will be done
in earth, as it is in Heaven."

Printed in the United States
By Bookmasters